GLOBAL
PERSPECTIVES ON
CHRISTIANITY

Case Studies to Promote Thinking Skills in Religious Education

Janet King

with

Brian Stanley and **Trevor** & **Margaret Cooling**

RMEP

RELIGIOUS AND MORAL EDUCATION PRESS

Religious and Moral Education Press
A division of SCM-Canterbury Press Ltd
A wholly owned subsidary of Hymns Ancient
& Modern Ltd
St Mary's Works, St Mary's Plain
Norwich, Norfolk NR3 3BH

First published 2001

ISBN 1 85175 273 0

The authors would like to thank Sue Hookway, Helen Kendrick,
Yvonne Logan-Winters and Lorraine Milmer for their helpful
comments on an early draft of the pack. Thanks are due also to
Ruth and David Cooper, Jonathan Kim, Alan Kirkland and
Siobhan Speirs for recording some of the songs, to Ruth
Bushnell for her help with information on Indian dance and to
Rosemary Cottingham for the pictures and video clips from
Burundi. They would also like to thank Wylva Davies for her
assistance with copyright and other research. However, the
authors take full responsibility for the views and information
contained herein.

Grateful acknowledgement is due to the Jerusalem Trust and to
The Pew Charitable Trusts of Philadelphia for their generous
support in the development of this publication. The opinions
expressed are those of the authors and do not necessarily
represent the views of the funding bodies.

The Stapleford Centre is an interdenominational charity which
produces materials and offers in-service courses to resource
the teaching of Christianity in schools. Full details of courses
and publications are available from:

The Stapleford Centre,
The Old Lace Mill,
Frederick Road,
Stapleford,
Nottingham, NG9 8FN
Tel: 0115 939 6270
Fax: 0115 939 2076
E-mail: **admin@stapleford-centre.org**
Website: **www.stapleford-centre.org**

Designed and typeset by Topics – The Creative Partnership,
Exeter
Illustrations by Clive Wakfer and Brian Platt

Printed in Great Britain by Brightsea Press, Exeter for
SCM-Canterbury Press Ltd, Norwich

Contents

Using this resource

CONTRIBUTION TO RELIGIOUS EDUCATION

This pack has been designed to make the following contributions to RE:

- to enhance knowledge and understanding of Christianity as a multicultural and global faith;

- to develop thinking skills through engagement with case studies from global Christianity;

- to promote attitudes and dispositions important to citizenship and spiritual, moral, social and cultural development;

- to encourage a reflective response to Christianity as a world religion.

The resource is designed to raise levels of achievement amongst 11 to 16 year olds by providing them with new material in the form of case studies that they will not have met before. Our aim is that encountering this material will stimulate challenging questions and promote thinking at depth. The case studies are presented to students on the photocopiable stimulus sheets in the book and on the CD-ROM included in the pack.

THE THEMES

The resource is divided into six main themes (see contents page and table on pages 6–7). These have been selected from recent research material (see page 9). Each theme offers case studies that raise questions and issues of great importance in the study of religion and which provide opportunities to learn *from* religion.

Each theme begins with:

- an overview of its content;

- a list of learning outcomes;

- a glossary of key terms.

Each theme offers three options for study, from which teachers select according to their own scheme of work. The table on pages 6–7 provides assistance in making this selection. Each option is a stand-alone block of material. It is recommended that teachers should usually select option 1 if only one option is to be used in any unit of work.

Each option includes the following elements:

- a summary of the content;

- a list of learning outcomes;

- a list of the resources provided in the pack that are required for teaching the material;

- a list of the additional support material available on the accompanying CD-ROM;

- ideas for an introductory discussion;

- ideas for a main activity;

- suggested student tasks at three levels;

- a suggested activity for 'gifted and talented' students;

- a reflection;

- photocopiable stimulus sheets.

This resource pack is not designed to give a comprehensive account of global Christianity. (The majority of the examples are taken from the Protestant tradition.) Rather, the case studies have been selected for the insights that they offer into the growth of Christianity as a global faith and for the thinking that they can stimulate. Each case study is used to focus students' attention on one or more key issues integral to understanding the relationship between Christianity as a universal faith and its expression in many different and particular cultures. The pack is not, therefore, designed to offer a course on Christianity, but rather to supplement and complement the basic information that students will acquire in their RE in primary and secondary school. It offers a flexible resource which teachers can adapt according to their own needs and circumstances.

THE CD-ROM

An important feature of this pack is the CD-ROM, which offers support material that cannot easily or economically be provided in printed form. The CD-ROM can be used in a number of ways:

- for teachers to consult for further background information;

- for students to consult for full-colour pictures and diagrams;

- for playing musical and oral recordings;

- for producing full-colour OHTs;

- for providing research material which can be used by students, particularly the more able.

A site licence for downloading material from the CD-ROM onto the school intranet is included in the purchase price of the pack. The site licence, operating instructions and contents list for the CD-ROM are printed on the inside front and back cover of this book.

Note on websites

Although the authors have done everything they can to check the accuracy, availability and content of the websites listed, they cannot take responsibility for changes that may have taken place since the time of writing. It is advised that websites are checked in advance of their use by students. Alternative websites can be found using appropriate key words in a search.

PROGRESSION

Two strategies towards progression are adopted in this resource.

1. The material dealt with becomes progressively more complex and demanding from Theme 1 through to Theme 6. The themes are in three pairs:

Themes 1 & 2: Christianity as a global and multicultural faith

Themes 3 & 4: Conversion, Christian faith and personal culture

Themes 5 & 6: Christianity and personal, social and global issues in a multicultural context

2. In each theme, the student tasks are organized at three levels. These reflect the levels suggested by the Qualifications and Curriculum Agency in their guidance on RE.

Levels 3–4 reflect the potential achievement of most students at the age of 11.

Levels 5–6 reflect the potential achievement of most students at the age of 14.

Levels 7–8 reflect the potential achievement of most students at the age of 16.

Levels 3–4 reflect a basic level of attainment in interacting with the material where tasks:

- are based on mastery of the basic content;

- give more emphasis to description;

- have more structure;

- require some basic evaluation, analysis or creativity.

At levels 5–6 and 7–8 the tasks are made more difficult by, for example:

- requiring engagement with more demanding content;

- being more open-ended and less structured;

- giving more emphasis to analysis, synthesis and evaluation;

- making more demands on creativity;

- engaging with more controversial material;

- using more than one source of evidence;

- demanding greater skill in organization and presentation of work;

- requiring students to weigh differing viewpoints

SYLLABUS LINKS

This table demonstrates how the material in this resource fits into the content, aims and objectives specified by syllabuses of Religious Education and school schemes of work. For each of the six themes in the pack the following information is given:

General Topic – commonly used in RE syllabuses to identify broad areas of study.

Key questions which summarize: (1) the main aim under the attainment target *learning about religions* (AT 1); and (2) the main aim under the attainment target *learning from religion* (AT 2). These two attainment targets are widely adopted in syllabuses.

RE Skills promoted through the activities and tasks in the theme.

Theme 1: Who are the Christians?

General Topic
- Christianity in the modern world

Key Question 1
- Why does Christianity thrive in some cultures and not in others?

Key Question 2
- How do I recognize a stereotype?

RE Skills
- Investigating diversity in the Christian faith
- Identifying causes for the growth/decline of Christianity
- Reflecting on stereotypes
- Understanding a point of view
- Analysing pictures
- Expressing ideas

Attitudes/Dispositions
- Appreciating an alternative view to one's own
- Recognizing our own tendency to hold stereotypes
- Awareness of our own assumptions and accepting challenges to pre-conceived ideas
- Valuing the benefits of cultural diversity

Syllabus Links
Option 1:
- World-wide Church
- Spread of Christianity: the facts and the reasons
- Christianity in different cultures

Option 2:
- The Church in England
- Christianity and modern culture
- Perceptions of the Church

Option 3:
- Christianity in a changing world
- Religion and national identity
- Christianity and multiculturalism
- Denominations: the Anglican Church world-wide
- Diversity

Theme 2: How do Christians express their faith?

General Topic
- Christian expression and practice in a multicultural world

Key Question 1
- How do Christians of different cultures express and practise their faith?

Key Question 2
- How important is my culture to my personal identity? How can I express my ideas to people of another culture?

RE Skills
- Investigating cultural influence
- Explaining a belief
- Analysing pictures, songs and prayers
- Evaluating the impact of Christianity on different cultures
- Expressing understanding
- Selecting key information
- Interpreting religious language

Attitudes/Dispositions
- Valuing another point of view
- Appreciating the challenge of cross-cultural communication
- Valuing diverse modes of communication

Syllabus Links
Option 1:
- Christianity as a multicultural faith
- Christian buildings
- Incarnation
- Cultural diversity

Option 2:
- Translating the Bible
- Art in Christianity
- Language in Christianity

Option 3:
- Christian worship
- Prayer
- Music in Christianity

Theme 3: Christianity spreads

General Topic
- Christian beliefs, behaviour, attitudes and lifestyle

Key Question 1
- Why do Christians evangelize?

Key Question 2
- How do I react to other people's attempts to persuade me of the truth of their beliefs?

RE Skills
- Evaluating the distinction between facts and beliefs
- Interpreting religious language
- Analysing the impact of visual images
- Communicating ideas and views in different forms
- Empathizing with someone from a different culture
- Investigating appropriate evidence
- Interpreting primary sources

Attitudes/Dispositions
- Valuing truth and the importance of seeking it
- Welcoming alternative views to one's own
- Challenging stereotypes
- Desiring co-operation with others

Syllabus Links
Option 1:
- Evangelism
- Truth: facts and beliefs
- Christian mission and Christian witness
- The Christian Gospel

Option 2:
- Leading figures in Christianity
- Christianity and colonialism
- Christianity in Africa
- Faith in action

Option 3:
- The modern missionary
- Christianity: an international movement
- Interdependence/partnership

Attitudes/Dispositions promoted through the theme. These particularly highlight the contribution that the material can make to the teaching of *Citizenship* and the promotion of *spiritual, moral, social and cultural development.*

Syllabus Links for each of the three options for the theme. These are listed using the language adopted in many syllabuses and schemes of work, and are designed so that teachers can recognize where the material will fit in with their current scheme of work.

Theme 4: Changing faith

General Topic
- Christian beliefs, behaviour, attitudes and lifestyle

Key Question 1
- What does conversion to Christianity mean?

Key Question 2
- How are my personal identity and my behaviour influenced by my beliefs, my culture and my peers?

RE Skills
- Investigating and evaluating a life story
- Interpreting religious language
- Reflecting on change in one's life
- Analysing case studies
- Communicating ideas in a variety of ways
- Reflecting on a controversial issue

Attitudes/Dispositions
- Valuing a different perspective from one's own
- Reflecting on the influences that shape oneself
- Valuing conflict resolution
- Appreciating commitment and acting on beliefs
- Affirming people's human rights
- Willingness to embrace controversial issues in an open manner

Syllabus Links
Option 1:
- Conversion
- Key figures in Christianity
- Responses to the Christian message
- Faith and cultural identity

Option 2:
- Conversion
- Key figures in Christianity
- Group identity
- Belonging
- Conflict and peace between religions
- Faith in action
- Living with difference

Option 3:
- Commitment
- Responses to suffering
- Persecution, forgiveness and reconciliation
- Conflict and peace between religions
- The Christian disciple: a modern martyr
- Human rights

Theme 5: Keeping body and soul together

General Topic
- Christianity and global issues: values in practice

Key Question 1
- What is the relationship between the spiritual and the material in Christianity?

Key Question 2
- How important is the spiritual dimension compared to the material dimension of my life?

RE Skills
- Relating beliefs to action
- Communicating a message
- Reflecting on one's own ideas and actions
- Expressing other people's views accurately
- Empathizing with another person
- Applying new ideas

Attitudes/Dispositions
- Willingness to consider a different view of life
- Valuing acting to achieve social justice
- Reflecting on the spiritual dimension

Syllabus Links
Option 1:
- Aid agencies and their work
- Jubilee 2000
- Christianity, wealth and materialism
- Responding to poverty and third world debt
- Christianity and social justice
- Applying the Bible
- Human rights

Option 2:
- Christian healing and medicine
- Christian belief about the nature of humans
- The meaning of salvation
- Values
- The spiritual and the material worlds

Option 3:
- Responses to suffering
- Key figures in Christianity
- Liberation theology
- Denominations: the Pentecostal churches
- Applying the Bible
- Human rights
- Social justice

Theme 6: Women, men and God

General Topic
- Christianity and social and personal issues: values in practice

Key Question 1
- How does Christian faith affect gender relationships?

Key Question 2
- For what do I value other people?

RE Skills
- Synthesizing western and non-western approaches
- Evaluating different points of view
- Reflecting on our own attitudes and values
- Applying unfamiliar information
- Empathizing with another person's situation
- Applying biblical texts
- Expressing ideas through imagery

Attitudes/Dispositions
- Attending to the views of others
- Living with ambiguity in moral dilemmas
- Valuing other human beings for who they are and not what they do
- Accepting challenges to one's own beliefs and values
- Respecting someone different from oneself

Syllabus Links
Option 1:
- People created in the image of God
- Views of the human being
- Views of women's roles
- Weddings, marriage and parenthood

Option 2:
- Views of marriage
- Cultural diversity within Christianity
- Values and human relationships

Option 3:
- Applying the Bible
- Making difficult ethical decisions
- Marriage
- Conflict resolution
- Socially and morally responsible behaviour

THE IMPORTANCE OF THINKING SKILLS IN THE STUDY OF GLOBAL CHRISTIANITY

Christianity has never been a religion of the western world only, and in the twenty-first century it is no longer such even primarily. Whereas in 1800 over 90% of the world's professing Christians lived in Europe or North America, today over 60% are found in what is conventionally known as the 'Third World' – Africa, Asia, Latin America, and the Pacific. Christianity is a global faith and ought to be presented as such in the classroom.

Edward de Bono has observed that one of the greatest obstacles to new learning is what students already know. The adage 'familiarity breeds contempt' captures the problem and is particularly acute when it comes to teaching Christianity. Many of our students think they know about Christianity and therefore cannot envisage that there is anything new to learn. And there is certainly no need ever to consider changing their attitudes!

This resource attempts to break through this trap by offering case studies from global Christianity that present new material which students will not have met before. This comes from research, previously unused in schools (see page 9). The Christian faith is studied out of its familiar context, as students encounter new case studies through primary sources such as pictures, stories and documents. These sources act as a stimulus to the students that will, it is hoped, provoke them to *stop and think*. The teaching ideas offered in the pack mediate this unfamiliar content with activities that enable students to engage with the issues and ideas that it raises. An encounter with this unfamiliar stimulus material unsettles misplaced confidence and is the first step to challenging the illusion of knowledge.

A troubling feature for many people is that Christianity, as does Islam, claims to be universal truth, good news for all humanity. Its relevance cannot be restricted to one nation or to one cultural group. Perhaps one of the most serious challenges confronting RE today is to help students appreciate and handle the conflicting claims of the different religions, particularly as they are encountering one another more directly than ever before. The issues and tensions arising from such encounters are likely to be of increasing importance for politics and society, and hence are, rightly, forcing themselves onto the agenda of education.

However, this is not to claim that there is a universal Christian culture. Dr D. T. Niles, a leading theologian from Sri Lanka in the mid-twentieth century, had this to say:

> The gospel is like a seed, and you have to sow it. When you sow the seed of the gospel in Palestine, a plant that can be called Palestinian Christianity grows. When you sow it in Rome, a plant of Roman Christianity grows. You sow the gospel in Great Britain and you get British Christianity. The seed of the gospel is later brought to America, and a plant grows of American Christianity. Now, when missionaries came to our lands they brought not only the seed of the gospel, but also their own plant of Christianity, flowerpot included! So, what we have to do is break the flowerpot, take out the seed of the gospel, sow it in our own cultural soil, and let our version of Christianity grow.

Attempts to transport plant and flowerpot as well as the seed are now widely acknowledged as mistaken. This pack attempts to illustrate how the different plants of Christianity come from the one seed without sharing the same flowerpot!

In order to be able to deal with the challenging issues raised by such intercultural studies, students will need to be trained to become critical thinkers. In his book *Teaching Thinking* (Continuum, 1998, page 9), Robert Fisher sums up the characteristics of a good thinker as follows:

> Ideal critical thinkers display a number of intellectual virtues. These include:
>
> 1. Seeking truth
> They care that their beliefs are true, and that their decisions are as far as possible justified. They show this by:
>
> (a) seeking alternatives (hypotheses, explanations, conclusions, plans, sources, ideas)
>
> (b) supporting views only to the extent they are justified
>
> (c) being well informed, including being informed by the views of others.
>
> 2. Being honest
> They care that their position and the positions of others are represented honestly. They show this by attending, by:
>
> (a) being clear about what they mean
>
> (b) maintaining a focus on the issue in question
>
> (c) seeking and offering reasons
>
> (d) considering all factors relevant to the situation
>
> (e) being aware of their own point of view
>
> (f) considering seriously other points of view.

3. Respecting others
They care about the dignity and worth of every person. They show this by:

(a)   *attentive listening to the views of others*
(b)   *avoiding scorn or intimidation of others*
(c)   *showing concern about the welfare of others.*

Fisher is emphasizing the importance of attitudes and dispositions for students who are to develop into critical thinkers. These are precisely the same attitudes and dispositions that will also contribute to spiritual, moral, social and cultural development as well as being at the heart of Citizenship education. In this resource we have sought to promote these attitudes and dispositions so that through their studies of global Christianity, students' personal development is promoted in ways which will, it is hoped, influence their approach to other studies in RE and their education in general.

THE PRACTICE OF THINKING SKILLS

The following thinking skills will be promoted through the use of this pack:

- *creative* – for example, generating new ideas, being imaginative;

- *information processing* – for example, locating relevant information, analysing and interpreting information and understanding concepts and ideas;

- *reasoning* – for example, supporting answers with reasons, making deductions and judgements based on evidence;

- *enquiry* – for example, asking appropriate questions, defining problems and predicting outcomes;

- *evaluation* – for example, developing criteria for making judgements, evaluating information.

THE PARTNER ORGANIZATIONS

This resource is the product of a partnership between:

- Religious and Moral Education Press;

- Currents in World Christianity;

- The Stapleford Centre.

Currents in World Christianity (CWC) is an international and interdisciplinary research project on the transformation of Christianity into a global religion during the twentieth century. The project ran from 1998 to 2001 and was based in the Centre for Advanced Religious and Theological Studies in the Faculty of Divinity at the University of Cambridge. It was funded by The Pew Charitable Trusts of Philadelphia, USA. CWC represents a marriage of two previously existing initiatives:

- the North Atlantic Missiology Project, set up in 1996 to examine the relationship between theory and praxis in Protestant missions from the North Atlantic world;

- the International Project on Evangelicalism and Globalization, a group of scholars concerned to relate the current proliferation of evangelical forms of Christianity to theories of globalization.

CWC thus retains an emphasis on critical inquiry into the history of modern Christian missions, but sets this theme in the context of the growth of indigenous expressions of Christianity during the twentieth century. CWC has organized conferences and seminars on both sides of the Atlantic, and many of the papers delivered at these events are being published in academic journals and collected volumes. For more information, see the project website at **www.divinity.cam.ac.uk/carts/cwc**, or, from 2002 onwards, consult the website of the Henry Martyn Centre for the Study of Mission and World Christianity at **www.martynmission.cam.ac.uk.**

The Stapleford Centre is a registered charity that supports the teaching of Christianity in schools. It does this in three main ways:

- by publishing resources that develop new approaches;

- by providing teacher training;

- by engaging in research programmes.

Collaboration with CWC on this project fulfils all three of these aims. It has enabled us to develop a publication that explores a topic that is poorly represented in RE lessons, namely the relationship between culture and Christian faith. Furthermore, we hope that it will contribute to a greater understanding of the potential that exists for students to *learn from* their study of Christianity. The insights that we have gained from this work will be incorporated in our INSET courses, both short courses and our Certificate, Diploma and MA distance-learning courses validated by the University of Nottingham.

Further information about The Stapleford Centre is available on our website at:
   www.stapleford-centre.org

Theme 1: **Who are the Christians?**

THEME OVERVIEW *In this theme, students study the composition of the Christian Church across the world. The aim of this study is to help students understand the way in which the Christian message creates a different response in different cultures. Students should therefore come to understand that Christianity, while being one faith, has very different expressions around the world. They will see that the Church is growing dramatically in many parts of the non-western world, but is static or in decline in much of the western world. This will reinforce the idea that Christianity is a global and multicultural faith, a global family, but that different cultures respond to it in different ways. It will also help challenge the widespread teenage perspective that the Church is universally irrelevant (based on their western experience) and thereby encourage them to revisit their own, often unexamined, assumptions.*

The material provided is:

Option 1: Christianity – a global faith?

Option 2: A case study: Decline in church membership in England

Option 3: A case study in globalization: How has Christianity changed?

LEARNING OUTCOMES

It is expected that, through using this material, students will:

- understand that Christianity is a global faith (Options 1 and 3);

- reflect on why Christianity thrives in certain cultures but not in others (Options 1 and 2);

- review their own ideas about the place of the Church in the modern world (Option 2);

- consider how our own restricted experience can easily create stereotypes in our view of other people (Option 1).

GLOSSARY

Anglicanism A global Christian denomination linked by history and pattern of worship to the Church of England. Bishops and synods (assemblies representing the whole church) govern Anglican churches. Anglican worship follows a liturgy (written prayers, congregational responses and readings from the Bible) derived more or less closely from the Book of Common Prayer. This has its ultimate origins in the first Prayer Book produced during the English Reformation in 1549, during the reign of Edward VI. Every ten years, all Anglican bishops meet for the Lambeth Conference, under the leadership of the Archbishop of Canterbury. The last Lambeth Conference took place in 1998.

Church of England The Anglican Church in England.

Globalization A term used to convey the idea that the world is getting 'smaller' in the sense that communications systems and economic networks are tying different countries and economies more and more closely together.

Stereotype A fixed idea considered to represent a particular kind of person. The most common stereotypes are racial, but there are many others, such as religious and sexual.

Option 1: **Christianity – a global faith?**

SUMMARY

The core material illustrates how the religious map of the world has changed in the last hundred years as Christianity has been transformed from being a mainly western faith into a global and multi-cultural religion.

LEARNING OUTCOMES

It is expected that, through using this material, students will:

- understand that Christianity is a global faith;

- reflect on why Christianity thrives in certain cultures but not in others;

- consider how our own restricted experience can easily create stereotypes in our view of other people.

RESOURCES REQUIRED

- Stimulus Sheet 1.1: Portrait of a 21st-century Christian (1 each, main activity)

- Stimulus Sheet 1.2: Distribution of world Christian membership by continent, 1900–2000 – pie charts (1 between two, main activity/student tasks)

- Stimulus Sheet 1.3: Map of the growth rate of Christianity (1 between two, main activity/student tasks)

EXTRA RESOURCES AVAILABLE ON CD-ROM

- Distribution of world Christian membership by continent, 1900–2000 (colour pie charts)

- Colour map of the growth rate of Christianity

- The Christian faith: a global religion

TEACHING STEPS

INTRODUCTORY DISCUSSION

1. Introduce the idea of the world as a global village. Invite suggestions from students about advances in technology, travel and communications that have made our world 'smaller', e.g. TV/radio/mobilephones/computers/ Internet/air travel. Ask students how many different countries are represented by the restaurants in their locality or nearest town. Students may be able to talk about countries they have visited. The aim of this discussion is to underline the fact that the world is a much smaller place than it used to be.

2. In groups, students can brainstorm examples of phenomena and companies that have spread from one country across the world, e.g. cricket, baseball, Coca-Cola, Nike, McDonald's, Nintendo, Walmart. Introduce the idea that in some cases this has resulted in exactly the same product appearing all over the world, e.g. McDonald's burgers. (Have any members of the class visited McDonald's in other countries and found any differences in the food?) In other cases there may be adaptation to the local culture. (For example, many Indian restaurants serve quite mild food in Britain.) What is good about this outward spread? What are the disadvantages?

3. Introduce the term globalization (see glossary).

MAIN ACTIVITY

1. Using Stimulus Sheet 1.1, students write down five points that describe their perception of a typical Christian. Things to think about include skin colour, age, class, nationality and gender. They should either sketch or write their ideas in the frame.

2. Bring the class together to share their ideas. Read them the following description and discuss how closely their ideas related to it:

   The 'typical' Christian of the twenty-first century would be between 20 and 30 years old, brown-skinned, poor, living in the 'third world' and very enthusiastic about their faith. They could be either male or female.

3. Introduce the concept of stereotypes and how new information and experience can change people's fixed ideas.

4. Allocate the student tasks and distribute the two Stimulus Sheets 1.2 and 1.3 (see colour versions on the CD-ROM). Explain that these sheets show how Christianity has grown rapidly in some parts of the world and declined in others. (Students may find access to an atlas helpful.)

5. Allow students time for a final brief discussion of their findings after they have completed the tasks. Review the following points:

- In the last 100 years Christianity has shifted from a mainly European, western religion to a global, multi-cultural faith.
- In most cases, though not all, Christianity has grown most rapidly in poorer countries.
- In countries that have a high standard of living, Christianity appears to be either in decline (e.g. Western Europe) or static (e.g. USA).
- In countries where a different religion is predominant (e.g. Islam), Christianity is making only slow progress.
- In some countries where there is opposition to Christianity and even persecution, the Church seems to grow. Why? Is it perhaps because Christianity gives people a purpose in life, something to live and, if necessary, die for?

6. Ask students what information most surprises them and what information is as they expected.

STUDENT TASKS

Level 3–4 Task
(standard achievement age 11)

Ask students to list the following:

- one place where Christianity has declined;
- one place where it has grown rapidly;
- one place where there has been little or no growth.

Ask them to select which of the following factors they think may have been important in the decline/lack of growth of Christianity in the West, giving reasons for their answers:

- increase in wealth;
- changes in society (attitudes, thinking, etc.);
- political changes;
- increase in travel/communication.

Ask them to consider which of these factors have been important in the increased growth of Christianity in some areas and to give a reason.

Level 5–6 Task
(standard achievement age 14)

Ask students to look for the following:

- three Muslim countries (e.g. Iran);
- three western countries (e.g. Britain);
- three communist countries (e.g. China) or ex-communist countries (e.g. Romania).

What patterns can they see in the growth/decline of Christianity? What reasons can they give for these patterns? Ask them to think about the following issues:

- wealth and poverty;
- social reasons (attitudes, thinking, etc.);
- political reasons;
- technology (travel, communication, etc.).

Which factor do students think is the most important? Why?

Level 7–8 Task
(standard achievement age 16)

Ask students to prepare a presentation on the growth/decline of Christianity in different parts of the world, giving reasons for the trends they detect. They should use different ways of presenting their material: graphs, diagrams, etc.

Gifted and Talented

Ask students to imagine they are contributing to a Church website on the growth/decline of Christianity. They should use the stimulus sheets and the extra material on the CD-ROM and should include:

- trends and reasons for them;
- different ways of presenting the information (diagrams, charts, etc.);
- issues that people logging on might want to raise;
- stereotyping.

Reflection (All levels)

Ask students to think back to their first image of a typical Christian and to consider the following questions. 'How has the work you have done affected this image, if at all?' 'Would you call your first view a stereotype?' 'Can you think of other groups of people of whom you hold a stereotyped view?'

STIMULUS SHEET 1.1:
Portrait of a 21st-century Christian

Distribution of world Christian membership by continent 1900–2000

Distribution 1900

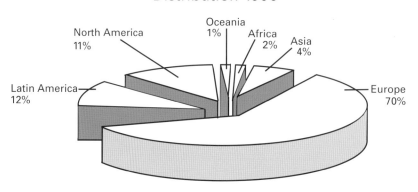

Distribution 1970

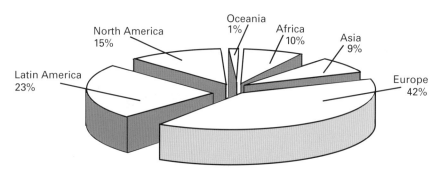

Distribution 2000

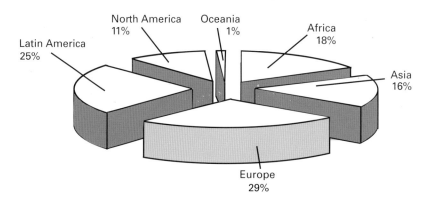

Statistics giving the breakdown of world Christian membership. Estimates (for 2001):

Roman Catholics 1,070,437,000   Other Protestants 346,650,000
Anglicans 80,717,000   Orthodox 216,247,000
Independent churches 394,102,000   Marginal Christians 26,526,000

(Source: *International Bulletin of Missionary Research*, January 2001, p. 25)

A colour version of these pie charts is available on the CD–ROM.

Map of the growth rate of Christianity

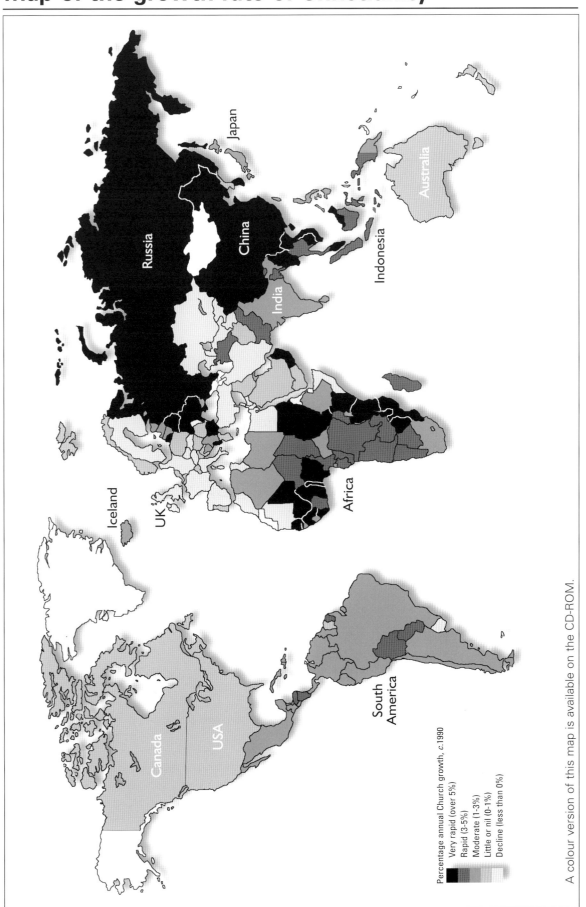

Percentage annual Church growth, c.1990

Very rapid (over 5%)
Rapid (3-5%)
Moderate (1-3%)
Little or nil (0-1%)
Decline (less than 0%)

A colour version of this map is available on the CD-ROM.

Theme 1: Who are the Christians?

Option 2: **A case study: Decline in church membership in England**

SUMMARY

This material draws on some of the evidence from a survey of patterns of church attendance in England that was carried out in 1998. The survey has given rise to a good deal of concern among English Christians. It highlights a decline in church attendance in England that is also typical of many other European countries.

LEARNING OUTCOMES

It is expected that, through using this material, students will:

- reflect on why Christianity thrives in certain cultures but not in others;

- review their own ideas about the place of the Church in the modern world.

RESOURCES REQUIRED

- Stimulus Sheet 1.4: Through the keyhole (1 each, introductory activity)

- Stimulus Sheet 1.5: A Church in crisis? (OHT or 1 per group, main activity)

- Stimulus Sheet 1.6: Some possible reasons for the decline in Sunday church attendance (1 per group, student tasks; the sheets should be cut up so that each group has a set of cards)

EXTRA RESOURCES AVAILABLE ON CD-ROM

- Websites illustrating the work and worship of a variety of churches

TEACHING STEPS

INTRODUCTORY DISCUSSION

1. Hand out Stimulus Sheet 1.4 and ask students to complete the sheet.

2. Ask students to work in pairs to compare their responses. As a pair they should produce one conclusion about the relevance of church services. This can be followed by a class discussion on the similarities and differences between their responses.

3. Explain that some people believe that the Church in Britain today is dying. Discuss whether this is true.

MAIN ACTIVITY

1. Give out Stimulus Sheet 1.5 or read it with students and discuss its implications. Things to think about include: church closure and its effect on the community; church schools; church voluntary work. (Note The line graph exercise should lead to a prediction of extinction in 2030. This assumes that decline continues at the same rate, which in fact is highly unlikely.)

2. Divide the class into six groups. Hand out the cut-up Stimulus Sheet 1.6, so that each group has a set of cards. Allocate student tasks.

STUDENT TASKS

Level 3–4 Task
(standard achievement age 11)

Ask each group to sort the cards into three piles according to their importance as factors in the decline in Sunday church attendance in Britain. They should be prepared to justify their choice as a group.

Pile 1 important
Pile 2 not so important
Pile 3 not at all important

Ask groups to consider, in the light of these factors, which two of the following suggestions they think might be crucial in improving church attendance:

- flexible timing (not always on a Sunday);
- services designed for different groups of people;
- better communications (e.g. using modern technology);
- making the message relevant to people's lives today.

Level 5–6 Task

(standard achievement age 14)

The task is the same as in level 3–4, but students should make other suggestions for improving Sunday attendance and rank the suggestions in order of effectiveness. They should justify their ranking.

Level 7–8 Task

(standard achievement age 16)

Ask students to imagine that they are researchers for a religious affairs programme. There is to be a programme about the decline in Sunday church attendance in Britain. They should:

- select the basic information on church decline that the programme planners will need;

- make suggestions for increasing church attendance (programme makers might want to explore these ideas);

- consider the likely success of these ideas (by making their own judgements and giving reasons for them and predicting other people's reactions to them).

Students should look at some of the church websites on the CD-ROM and draw on their own ideas to put together a briefing paper.

Gifted and Talented

In addition to the task for Level 7–8, students might like to put together an outline of the programme using a page split vertically – the commentary on one side, what is on screen on the other.

Reflection (All levels)

Statistics show that 7.5% of the population of the UK is in church on a Sunday. Ask students to consider what might draw these people to church even when the whole tide is against their going. Can they suggest what would draw *them* to something that was not a popular activity?

(**Note** The 7.5% is not evenly distributed: figures for Northern Ireland are higher.)

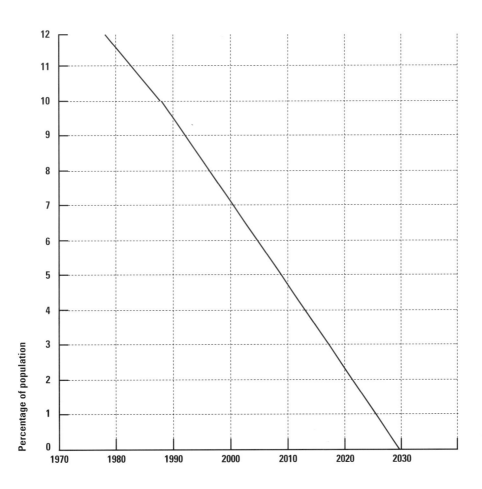

Line graph for Stimulus Sheet 1.5

STIMULUS SHEET 1.4
'Through the keyhole'

Look through the three keyhole views of what is taking place in three very different churches. In each of the corresponding boxes below, write a sentence explaining what you think is happening.

Complete one of the two sentences below:

I think church services are important because

I think church services are not important because

A Church in crisis?

Many people in Britain today believe that Christianity is dying. Many Church leaders believe that the Church in Britain is in crisis. In December 1998, the Archbishop of Canterbury said that the Church was in danger of 'bleeding to death' because so many people were leaving.

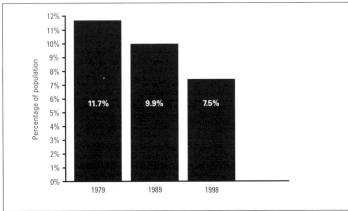

In a book called *The Tide Is Running Out,* the author, Dr Peter Brierley, records the results of his 1998 survey of English Church attendance. According to the survey, 11.7% of the population in England attended church on an average Sunday in 1979. In 1989 this figure had dropped to 9.9% and by 1998 the figure had become 7.5%.

Draw a line graph to predict when the Church will cease to exist if this decline continues.

"*I know I never come to church, but I often visit your website!*"

Theme 1: **Who are the Christians?**

19

STIMULUS SHEET 1.6
Some possible reasons for the decline in Sunday church attendance

People prefer to go shopping on Sundays instead of going to church.

If people want a church service they watch it on the TV or on the web.

People don't like going to church because they think the people there will disapprove of them – for example, if they are living together but are not married.

There are lots of sports to play and watch on Sundays.

People are too busy.

There are more people of other faiths, so fewer people go to church.

No one wants to be seen going to church by their friends!

Sunday is for relaxing, lying in bed and catching up with jobs (like doing homework due in on Monday morning).

There are more interesting things to go to at church in the week, like youth club. So some people go to these activities instead of going on Sundays.

Families do things together on Sundays, so there is no time for church.

Going to church is not the 'expected thing to do', as it used to be years ago.

People say: 'You don't have to go to church to be a Christian.'

Option 3: **How has Christianity changed?**

SUMMARY

This material looks at a significant change that has taken place in the Anglican Church (see glossary) as a case study of how Christianity has changed from being a mainly European/western religion to being a global, multi-cultural faith.

LEARNING OUTCOME

It is expected that, through using this material, students will:

- understand that Christianity is a global faith.

RESOURCES REQUIRED

- Stimulus Sheet 1.7: 'Call me an Anglican' (OHT or 1 between two, main activity)

- Stimulus Sheet 1.8: The Lambeth Conference, 1867 and 1998 (1 between two, main activity/student tasks)

- Stimulus Sheet 1.9: Illustrations from the Lambeth Conference 1867 and 1998 (1 between two, main activity/student tasks)

EXTRA RESOURCES AVAILABLE ON CD-ROM

- Article: 'Anglican' or 'English'?

- Lambeth Conference photos from 1867 and 1998

TEACHING STEPS

INTRODUCTORY DISCUSSION

1. Discuss with students the way in which games that originated in Europe have spread across the world – for example, cricket from England, golf from Scotland. Comparisons might be made with other sports where 'globalization' has taken place. Football is a good example of this. For instance, a premier league club may regularly field a team with many 'foreign' players and the current manager of the English team comes from Sweden. Why has this happened? Is it a good thing? Encourage students to give reasons for their responses.

2. Explain that this work focuses on how Christianity, which in the past appeared to be very closely associated with western culture, has now become a global religion. In this option students will look at the Anglican Church and its change from being essentially an English export to what is now a global church. (For definitions of 'Anglican' and 'Church of England' see the glossary and the CD-ROM article.)

MAIN ACTIVITY

1. Give out Stimulus Sheet 1.7 or display it on the OHP. Explain the difference between the terms 'Anglican Church' and 'Church of England' (see CD-ROM), as reflected in the Stimulus Sheet. Option: ask students to suggest a diagram to express the difference between 'Anglican' and 'English'.

2. Hand out Stimulus Sheets 1.8 and 1.9 and explain what the 'Lambeth Conference' is (see notes on Sheet 1.8).

3. Allocate the student tasks. Make sure that students are aware of the following points:

   (a) The lack of black or brown faces in the first photograph.
   (b) The growth in the numbers attending the 1998 Conference compared to 1867.
   (c) The number of black and coloured delegates attending the 1998 Conference.
   (d) The presence of a few women Bishops at the 1998 Conference.

4. Afterwards, bring the class back together to share findings.

STUDENT TASKS

Level 3–4 Task

(standard achievement age 11)

Ask students to compare the two photographs and details of the 1867 and 1998 Lambeth Conferences. What are the differences and similarities? Which of these do they think are important and why? They should imagine that a delegate from the 1867 conference could time-travel to the 1998 conference. What would be familiar? What would be strange to the delegate? How do they think a delegate from 1867 would feel about the changes that have occurred? They should give reasons for their answers.

Level 5–6 Task

(standard achievement age 14)

Ask students to imagine an 1867 delegate talking to a 1998 delegate. What questions do they think the 1867 delegate would want to ask the 1998 delegate? Students should list their questions and write down some responses the delegate might get. They could then turn the ideas into a taped interview. They should also write down their response to the two photographs.

Level 7–8 Task

(standard achievement age 16)

Ask students to compare and contrast the two photographs of the Lambeth Conferences. They should write an article for a broadsheet newspaper, in the appropriate style, pointing out the main differences between the conferences. They should give opinions on why these changes have occurred and assess them. Are the changes for the better? A suitable headline will be needed for the article, i.e. one that reflects the differences.

Gifted and Talented

Students can pose a number of questions they think are raised by having a church that spreads across the world. These can be turned into 'key questions' that the group can discuss on another occasion.

Reflection (All levels)

The symbol of the Anglican Church is the compass rose, chosen because it points to all the corners of the earth. (See the illustration on Stimulus Sheet 1.8.) Ask students to design their own symbol to express their understanding of the global nature of the Anglican Church.

STIMULUS SHEET 1.7
'Call me an Anglican'

Two hundred years ago, the terms 'the Church of England' and 'the Anglican Church' meant much the same thing. So to be a member of the Anglican Church implied simply that you had been born and baptized into the established Church of the English nation. However, today, being 'English' and being 'Anglican' are no longer identical ideas.

"I am a leader in the Anglican church in the town where I live in South Africa. As an Anglican, I accept the teaching of my church. This does not mean that I have lost or given up my African cultural roots and identity. This is reflected in the way we worship God and in the way we interpret the teachings of Jesus within our community. My 'hero' is Desmond Tutu, who became the first black Anglican Archbishop of Cape Town in 1986. I think it would be good if the next Archbishop of Canterbury was not English and was black."

"I am an Anglican and I work with the children in my local Church of England church. The Church of England has changed a lot in the last few years as a result of many changes in society. I too think it would be good for the global Anglican Church if we had a leader who represented the wider Anglican community. Perhaps it could be someone from a third-world country where Christianity is on the increase?"

TASK

Both these people are members of the Anglican Church but they come from very different backgrounds and cultures. What do you think of the idea of an African Archbishop of Canterbury?

It is not a new idea. In the seventh century Adrian the African declined the invitation to become Archbishop, but he did become Abbot of Canterbury. The job of Archbishop went to Theodore, who came from the area we now call Turkey.

Think of reasons for and against having an African Archbishop of Canterbury.

STIMULUS SHEET 1.8
The Lambeth Conference, 1867 and 1998

The Lambeth Conference is a gathering of all the bishops in the Anglican Church. It takes place every ten years in England and is led by the Archbishop of Canterbury.

The first Lambeth Conference was held in 1867. Seventy-six bishops attended this first conference. The record of those in attendance reveals that some bishops came from parts of the non-western world but by far the largest groups came from the UK and North America. These are some of the places represented at that first conference.

- **Jamaica**
- **United Kingdom**
- **Sierra Leone**
- **China and Japan**
- **Canada**
- **Cape Town**
- **Gibraltar**
- **India**
- **Barbados**
- **Honolulu**
- **Jerusalem**
- **New Zealand**
- **Bombay**
- **United States**

The number of bishops attending these conferences has grown enormously over the years. In 1998 the conference was held at Kent University and 1500 people attended from every corner of the world. It was the largest ever Lambeth Conference. In 1998 the numbers of bishops attending were:

- **224 from Africa (the largest delegation)**
- **177 from North America**
- **139 from the United Kingdom and Europe**
- **95 from Asia**
- **56 from Australia, New Zealand and Oceania**
- **41 from Central America**
- **4 from the Middle East**

Comparing the pictures taken of the bishops attending the 1998 Lambeth Conference with pictures taken of the 76 bishops attending in 1867, reveals that the Church of England now makes up only a small, and in many ways unrepresentative, minority of the global Anglican Church.

SOMETHING TO THINK ABOUT

Lamin Sanneh, Professor of Missions and World Christianity at Yale University, has estimated that since the 1960s the Church in Africa has grown from 60 million to over 300 million members.

The symbol of the Anglican Church is the compass rose.

STIMULUS SHEET 1.9
The Lambeth Conference, 1867 and 1998

1867

1998

These photographs are available on the CD-ROM.

Theme 2: How do Christians express their faith?

THEME OVERVIEW *In this theme, students focus on the relationship between culture and Christianity. The material provided looks at the different ways in which Christians around the world express their faith. Students are introduced to the idea that the Christian faith can be 'translated', so that the message is preserved but expressed in forms that are culturally relevant.*

Christians believe that God took on the form of a man (Jesus) in a particular culture (first-century Palestine). This belief is called incarnation. Students are introduced to this idea.

The material provided is:

Option 1: Can Christianity be expressed in any culture?

Option 2: Putting the Bible into words

Option 3: Christian worship in different cultures

LEARNING OUTCOMES

It is expected that, through using this material, students will:

- understand that Christianity has spread through the principle of 'translatability' (Options 1, 2 and 3);

- understand the basic Christian doctrine of the incarnation (Option 1);

- reflect on how the principle of the 'translatability' of the Christian faith is expressed in different styles of art and architecture, in different versions of the Bible and in a variety of forms of worship around the world (Options 1, 2 and 3);

- consider which aspects of their own culture can be translated into other forms (Option 3);

- reflect on the importance of culture in their own life and the significance of cultural change and culture shock (Option 1).

GLOSSARY

Ashram A place set up for spiritual development (usually by Hindus), often associated with a particular guru (spiritual teacher); mostly found in India.

Culture The system of beliefs, values and practices which binds a society together and gives it a sense of identity and security. Sometimes described as 'the way we do things round here'.

Globalization A term used to convey the idea that the world is getting 'smaller' in the sense that communications systems and economic networks are tying different countries and economies more and more closely together.

Incarnation In Christianity this means God becoming a human being in the person of Jesus.

Localization A term used to describe the tendency, in response to globalization, of local communities to become more concerned about preserving their own identities.

Option 1: Can Christianity be expressed in any culture?

SUMMARY

The core material reviews the concept of globalization (see Theme 1) and introduces the idea of localization. It then goes on to examine how Christianity has become global, but in a way that is sensitive to 'local' cultures. The concept of incarnation is introduced. The material emphasizes the idea that there are many different ways of being Christian in the world today.

LEARNING OUTCOMES

It is expected that, through using this material, students will:

- understand that Christianity has spread through the principle of 'translatability';

- understand the basic Christian doctrine of the incarnation;

- reflect on how the principle of the 'translatability' of the Christian faith is expressed in different styles of art and architecture and in a variety of forms of worship around the world;

- reflect on the importance of culture in their own life and the significance of cultural change and culture shock.

RESOURCES REQUIRED

- Stimulus Sheet 2.1: The culture bowl (1 each, main activity)

- Stimulus Sheet 2.2: Places of worship (1 between two, student tasks)

- Stimulus Sheet 2.3: Out of Africa (1 between two, student tasks)

EXTRA RESOURCES AVAILABLE ON CD-ROM

- Repeat pictures of church buildings in Asia and Africa (Stimulus Sheet 2.2)

- Repeat pictures from the 'Out of Africa' sheet (Stimulus Sheet 2.3)

- Websites on the Amish

- Video clips and photos of the Anglican Church at worship in Burundi

TEACHING STEPS

INTRODUCTORY DISCUSSION

1. Review the work on globalization (Theme 1). Ask how many students like McDonald's. Then ask if anyone has been abroad and visited a McDonald's in another country. What did they notice? Make the point that, while the buildings are similar and hamburgers and French fries are universal, in some countries there are other choices on the menu which attempt to take into account cultural preferences in food. In fact, McDonald's are now including fast food from other countries, e.g. China, on their menus.

2. Talk about the 'McDonaldization', or the 'Cocacola-ization', of society that has taken place and the fact that globalization has made the world a smaller place. Modern technology and communications systems mean that ideas can be spread across the globe very quickly. List the issues this phenomenon raises. This can be followed up in discussion if time permits.

3. Remind the students that there are also cultural differences. Ask them for examples of places they have visited where aspects of the local culture have seemed very strange to them. Introduce the concept of 'localization' (see glossary).

4. Explain that globalization and localization can be seen in Christianity. There are aspects of Christianity that remain constant across the world, but at the same time people express their faith in a variety of different ways that make sense to them in their own cultural contexts. Christians are the same, yet different.

MAIN ACTIVITY

1. Introduce the idea of different cultures. Explain that culture is something that we take for granted but which is essential to our life. A good analogy is that culture is to human beings as water is to fish. (Students may be able to suggest their own analogies.) Explain the concept of 'culture shock', something that

people experience when they enter a culture that is very different from their own. In the same way that a fish out of water is left gasping, someone placed in a different culture can find themselves feeling very upset.

2. Culture becomes visible in things like body language, clothing, food, entertainment and so on. Ask students to think of the things that are part of their culture. Give them Stimulus Sheet 2.1 and ask them to complete the activity. Have they ever experienced culture shock? Would their parents experience culture shock if they were taken to any of the students' social events? Ask for reasons for their responses.

3. Introduce the concept of incarnation. Christians believe that when God became a human being in Jesus, he did it in a way that avoided 'culture shock' by ensuring that he became an ordinary human being and not a 'Superman' type of figure. So he was born into a particular culture at a particular time in history. Jesus was a first-century Jew. But as time went on lots of different people became his followers. Each of these followers expressed their faith in their own culture; they did not have to try to live as first-century Jews in order to be Christians. Ask students to imagine how Jesus might have been different if he had come to twenty-first-century Britain.

4. Explain that a mistake that has sometimes been made is that people forget that the Christian faith can be expressed in different cultures. As a result, Christians sometimes share not only their faith, but also their culture. Ask students to imagine the Christian faith as a seed and culture as the soil in which it grows. If you sow the 'seed' of the gospel in 'American soil', you get the 'plant' of American Christianity. If you sow the 'seed' of the gospel in 'Indian soil' you get the 'plant' of Indian Christianity. The problem is that sometimes Christians want to take their own plant (and even the flowerpot!) to another culture rather than just the 'seed' (see page 8). Students may wish to develop their own analogy.

5. Hand out Stimulus Sheets 2.2 and 2.3 and allocate the student tasks. Use material from the CD-ROM as appropriate.

STUDENT TASKS

Level 3–4 Task

(standard achievement age 11)

Ask students to consider in what ways the examples on Stimulus Sheet 2.3 express Christian beliefs through African culture. Ask them to consider how the Christians from Taiwan and Uganda have

expressed their culture and their Christian faith in the way they have built their churches (see Sheet 2.2).

Level 5–6 Task

(standard achievement age 14)

Ask students to look at Stimulus Sheet 2.3 and consider how African Christians have expressed their faith in a way that is culturally appropriate. What beliefs are expressed in these examples that are common to many Christians? Using Stimulus Sheet 2.2, students should imagine that a new church is being built in their area. How could the church reflect their local culture? Points to take into account:

- what is important to the people of the area;
- local industry, environment and history;
- how the Christian message can be linked with these things.

Students should write/draw some suggestions in a letter to a local architect.

Level 7–8 Task

(standard achievement age 16)

'Christianity is just a means of spreading western culture.' Students should write arguments both defending and attacking this idea, using the image of the seed (Christian faith) and soil (culture). They should draw on examples from both stimulus sheets to illustrate their arguments.

Gifted and Talented

Using the stimulus sheets, students should assess the degree to which African and Asian Christians have successfully integrated and expressed their faith and their culture. They should use what they have learned to evaluate other Christian groups – for example, the Amish. (The Amish are a Christian group of North Americans who maintain a culture, language and dress of another age and another continent as an essential part of their Christianity.) Websites on the Amish are listed on the CD-ROM.

Reflection (All levels)

Either Discuss the idea that we can experience culture shock in many ways: moving between countries, age groups and social classes. Culture shock can be an unpleasant experience, but it can also be a way in which we learn from other cultures and begin to question our own assumptions. Ask students in what ways they think that *some degree* of culture shock could be a beneficial experience.

Or Ask students to think about some of the things we take for granted which might change in another culture. Which aspect of life would they have most difficulty changing? Ask them to think for a moment about the changes that some people have to go through when they enter western culture.

STIMULUS SHEET 2.1
The culture bowl

Culture is made up of:

- **the way we think**
- **body language/ gestures**
- **things we take for granted**
- **language**
- **dress**
- **food**
- **behaviour**
- **music and the arts**
- **beliefs**
- **political systems**
- **family life**

For example, in early twenty-first century western culture many of us take for granted democracy, freedom of choice, and the ability to choose our own marriage partners. These things are part of our 'culture'.

ACTIVITY

Imagine you have been moved out of your own culture and into another one where many of the factors listed above are different. Under each label below write down how that part of life may be different. For example, think of the way you dress now. In another culture how might that change? Which of the changes would you find most difficult to adapt to?

Things we take for granted

Language

Dress

Food

Behaviour

Music and the arts

Beliefs

Political systems

Family life

Body language/gestures

Entertainment

STIMULUS SHEET 2.2
Places of worship

Yayu village Presbyterian Church, Orchid Island, Taiwan

The boat (tatala) on the front of the church represents fishing, which is the main occupation of the people of Yayu. Over the door is the symbol of the Presbyterian Church – the burning bush. This symbol indicates that the church is a place to talk to God, for God spoke to Moses from a burning bush (Exodus 3). The two circles on the front of the church are the 'eyes' that are often painted on the sides of the fishing boats. The feathery patterns on the ends of the boats are traditional symbols for people.

Christ Church, Cawnpore, India

This church, completed in 1840, was built by Victorians in an English style. It contrasts dramatically with the Indian building in the background.

The Third Cathedral at Namirembe, Uganda

This church, built in 1901, is nothing like an English cathedral. The Victorians did not always build in English styles.

These pictures are also available on the CD-ROM.

STIMULUS SHEET 2.3
Out of Africa

Over the years, some (though certainly not all) Christians have tried to make people from other cultures conform to their culture. They tended to assume that the only way of being a Christian was, for example, to follow British culture. The following examples demonstrate a different approach.

I have no words to thank you

O my Father, Great Elder,
I have no words to thank you
But with your deep wisdom
I am sure that you can see
How I value your glorious gifts.
O my Father, when I look upon
your greatness,
I am confounded with awe.
O Great Elder,
Ruler of all things earthly
and heavenly,
I am your warrior,
Ready to act in accordance
with your will.

Kikuyu, Kenya

Bishop Nehemiah Gotore ordaining Sauro Garanuako as bishop of the Zion Sabbath Church

Ethiopian church drummer

Christian dance in Burundi

God is part of the African past. He is not something new, imported by Europeans. Each African group of people had their own name for the Creator. The first missionaries recognized that the African idea of a powerful creator echoed the God of the Bible. The Mende people called God Ngewo; the Yoruba people called him Olorun. So the missionaries took the name Ngewo or Olorun for the God of the Bible.

These pictures are also available on the CD-ROM.

Option 2: **Putting the Bible into words**

SUMMARY

This material focuses on the importance of the Bible to Christians and their commitment to making it available for people to read in their own language. Christians believe that the Bible should be translated so that people can not only read it in their own language but also relate to the cultural setting, thus enabling anyone to understand its meaning.

LEARNING OUTCOMES

It is expected that, through using this material, students will:

- understand that Christianity has spread through the principle of 'translatability';

- reflect on how the principle of the 'translatability' of the Christian faith is expressed in different styles of art and in different versions of the Bible around the world.

RESOURCES REQUIRED

- Different versions of the Bible (1 per group, introduction)

- Stimulus Sheet 2.4: Language lines (1 between two, main activity)

- Stimulus Sheet 2.5: A painting from Asia (1 between two, main activity/ student tasks)

- Stimulus Sheet 2.6: A painting from Asia (1 between two, main activity/ student tasks)

EXTRA RESOURCES AVAILABLE ON CD-ROM

- Website addresses for Bible Society and Wycliffe Bible Translators

- Psalm 23 being sung in Kirundi (video)

- John 3:16 in three languages

- Colour version of two Asian paintings

- Chinese painting of the Annunciation

- A cartoon story of a translation problem

- More examples of translation problems

- Article from the *Christian Herald*

- List of translations of the Bible

TEACHING STEPS

INTRODUCTORY DISCUSSION

1. Show students various translations of the Bible, ranging from the Authorized Version to modern versions in everyday speech. A Bible or New Testament in another language would also be helpful. See Psalm 23 and John 3:16 on the CD-ROM.

2. Choose a suitable verse to be read out from different versions so that students can hear how they differ. A variety of translations are listed on the CD-ROM.

3. Talk about why Christians feel it is important for people to read the Bible in their own language and in a form that makes sense in their own culture. Explain that they don't want it to be a culture shock when people read the Bible for the first time. Illustrate this concern by using Psalm 23 on the CD-ROM. This task is not just a matter of getting the right words. It also requires some creativity in finding local equivalents to biblical terms and concepts, so that the words make sense to the reader.

4. Mention the work of organizations like the Bible Society and the Wycliffe Bible Translators. Website addresses can be found on the CD-ROM.

5. Explain the difference between Christianity and Islam in this respect. In the Islamic faith, the divine inspiration and authority of the Qur'an are linked to the original Arabic language in which it was revealed and later written. The Qur'an, unlike the Bible, cannot legitimately be translated into other languages.

MAIN ACTIVITY

1. Hand out Stimulus Sheet 2.4 or copy it on to an OHT. Ask students to complete the tasks. Extra examples of translation problems can also be found on the CD-ROM.

2. Give out Stimulus Sheets 2.5 and 2.6. The paintings can be seen in colour on the CD-ROM.

3. Ask students to read the story of Jesus washing the disciples' feet (John 13:2–17).

4. Allocate the student tasks, and after they are completed, bring students together to share findings.

STUDENT TASKS

Level 3–4 Task

(standard achievement age 11)

Ask students to imagine they are one of the artists staying at Jyoti's ashram. They see Jyoti working on his painting 'Washing the Feet'. What questions might they want to ask the artist about this story and the way that he is portraying it? Questions should cover meaning and significance as well as content. These questions can be followed up in discussion.

Level 5–6 Task

(standard achievement age 14)

Ask students to compare and contrast the two paintings. They should consider in what ways the artists have been faithful to both the text of the story and to their own culture, and give evidence for their answers.

Level 7–8 Task

(standard achievement age 16)

Ask students to compare and contrast the two paintings and to list the ways in which the culture of each artist is reflected in the paintings (medium, style, dress, gesture, etc.). They should imagine that they have been asked to paint a picture of the Christmas story (Matthew 1:18–2:12; Luke 2:1–20) for their town in a way that will reflect the local culture. Using what they have learned about drawing on local culture from the two artists, they should create a rough sketch, with notes, for their own painting.

Gifted and Talented

Students should look at the Chinese painting of the Annunciation on the CD-ROM, as well as the two Asian paintings on Stimulus Sheets 2.5 and 2.6 and answer the following questions:

- What Christian beliefs are reflected in the paintings?

- What are the challenges of being both true to the culture and true to Christian beliefs?

Reflection (All levels)

Ask students to think of a situation where they might have to work hard to communicate – for example, explaining to a grandparent how to use a computer. How would they do it in a way that makes sense and at the same time does not patronize the person? Discuss how easy it is for misunderstandings to arise or for people to be made to feel stupid.

STIMULUS SHEET 2.4
Language lines

Many words do not translate easily from one language into another. Translators have to search for the word that, as nearly as possible, has the same *inner* meaning as the original.

When Jesus said:

'Let not your hearts be troubled ...' (John 14:1)

he was using the term 'heart' to refer to the 'real me'. But for some people of the northern Congo, the 'real me' resides not in the heart but in the liver. Hence Bible translators have had to translate this verse as:

'Let not your livers be troubled ...'!

TASK

Imagine that the Bible is being translated for a tribe of South American (Amazonian) Indians. Some of the words or phrases in the following extracts might be difficult for these people to understand.

- 'Though your sins are like scarlet they shall be as white as snow.' (Isaiah 1:18)

- 'I am sending you out like sheep into the midst of wolves.' (Matthew 10:16)

- Then he [Jesus] said to them, 'Give to Caesar what is Caesar's and to God what is God's.' (Matthew 22:21)

- There on the poplars (willows) we hung our harps. (Psalm 137:2)

(a) Say why it would be impossible or meaningless to translate every word in these sentences literally.

(b) Suggest alternative words or phrases (in English) which might convey the inner meaning of the original.

STIMULUS SHEET 2.5
A painting from Asia

THINGS TO THINK ABOUT

- What story does the picture tell?

- Make links with what you already know to explore the meaning of the picture.

- Look for symbols. What do you think they mean?

- What questions do you want to ask about the painting?

- What feelings does the painting evoke?

'Washing the Feet' by Jyoti Sahi

Information about the artist

Jyoti Sahi is an influential Christian artist in Bangalore, India. He explores the relationship between art and culture. He is anxious that art should not be something objective that people merely observe, but something people get involved in, something that speaks to the present. Jyoti Sahi lives in an ashram, living and painting there with fellow artists. (An ashram is a place which is set aside for people to meet together to pursue spiritual matters.)

This painting can be viewed on the CD–ROM.

Jyoti Sahi is not interested in just preserving an ancient Indian art form – something that attracts tourists. He wants authentic Asian expression of the Christian way of looking at the world, not just something that appears superficially Asian. He is particularly interested in the links between Christianity and the ancient Indian religions. This has been well represented in his art and is evident in this painting. It shows Jesus washing a disciple's feet within the shape and outline of a leaf from the sacred Bodhi tree. (This is the tree under which the Buddha became enlightened.)

Theme 2: How do Christians express their faith?

35

STIMULUS SHEET 2.6
A painting from Asia

THINGS TO THINK ABOUT

- What story does the picture tell?

- Make links with what you already know to explore the meaning of the picture.

- Look for symbols. What do you think they mean?

- What questions do you want to ask about the painting?

- What feelings does the painting evoke?

'Jesus washes Peter's feet' by Sadao Watanabe

Information about the artist

When asked about his art, Watanabe said 'I wanted to find a way of expressing my Christianity within a Japanese context instead of just adapting the European tradition.'

He used a particular form of printing called *katazome*, which involved dyeing through a cut-paper stencil using a technique that had been traditional in the Okinawan Islands for several hundred years. For both his stencils and his prints, Watanabe used paper hand-made from the bark of the mulberry tree.

Not only did he use the simplicity of Japanese folk art to communicate the Christian message, but also his settings have aspects that are uniquely Japanese. Sometimes the disciples wear kimonos and in one print Peter is dressed as a Samurai. Some of Watanabe's prints reflect the work of Buddhist artists; for example, the long fingers of his figures are expressive, as in Buddhist icons.

This painting can be viewed on the CD-ROM.

Option 3: Christian worship in different cultures

SUMMARY

This material introduces students to some hymns and prayers from around the world. They are asked to consider the way in which the people who use them understand God, Jesus and themselves in relation to the Christian faith. This material will help students locate the various hymns and prayers in their cultural context.

LEARNING OUTCOMES

It is expected that, through using this material, students will:

- understand that Christianity has spread through the principle of 'translatability';

- reflect on how the principle of the 'translatability' of the Christian faith is expressed in different styles of art and architecture, in different versions of the Bible and in a variety of forms of worship around the world;

- consider which aspects of their own culture can be translated into other forms.

RESOURCES REQUIRED

- Stimulus Sheet 2.7: Prayers from around the world (1 between two, student tasks)

- Stimulus Sheet 2.8: Songs from around the world (1 between two, main activity/student tasks)

EXTRA RESOURCES AVAILABLE ON CD-ROM

- Teacher information – Prayer, music and dance in Christian worship

- Recordings of the songs on Stimulus Sheet 2.8

- Extra songs from Africa and India ('Tanglaw' and 'Light Has Come')

- The Sussex carol ('On Christmas morn all Christians sing')

- Extra prayers

- Indian Christian dance video clip

- African Christian dance from Burundi

- Song – 'Siyahamba' ('Marching in the Light')

- Notes on Indian dance from 'God's Everywhere People'

TEACHING STEPS

INTRODUCTORY DISCUSSION

1. Explain that the class will be looking at prayer, music and dance. Discuss which of these things are important in student culture today and why.

2. Explain the importance of prayer, music and dance in Christian worship (see teacher information on the CD-ROM). Play the song 'Siyahamba' ('Marching in the Light') and the Sussex carol as examples of different types of music associated with dance.

3. The video of Indian Christian dance demonstrates dance in a non-western culture. 'God's Everywhere People' contains material about Indian dance. Teachers may wish to show this to illustrate the use of dance. African dance used in worship can also be viewed. All this material is available on the CD-ROM.

MAIN ACTIVITY

1. Listen to some of the recordings of the songs on the CD-ROM. Choose one or more songs and ask students to identify key characteristics, such as the speed, the rhythm, words, mood, etc. Which country do they think the music comes from? What are their first reactions? How did the music make them feel? Why do they think it was created?

2. Hand out Stimulus Sheet 2.8. Ask different groups to choose different songs and create a summary of the message or beliefs contained within the song. They should also describe how the music helps to communicate that message.

3. Allocate student tasks, and after they have completed them, bring students back together to share their findings.

Note Students who come from different cultures may be willing to share their own experiences in this area.

STUDENT TASKS

Level 3–4 Task

(standard achievement age 11)

Ask students to imagine that a CD entitled 'Global Christian Worship' is being made. They should choose four items, two prayers and two songs, from Stimulus Sheets 2.7 and 2.8 to include on the CD, giving reasons for their choices. Ask them to design a CD cover that incorporates cultural images suitable for the prayers/songs.

Level 5–6 Task

(standard achievement age 14)

Using Stimulus Sheet 2.7, students should choose four prayers (more are available on the CD-ROM if required) and for each one:
- identify the theme and key ideas expressed in the prayer;
- locate the country of origin on the map;
- explain how it reflects both the culture and the faith of the writer.

Level 7–8 Task

(standard achievement age 16)

Ask students to look back over the prayers and songs on the Stimulus Sheets. If possible they should view the Indian and African dance and listen to some of the music on the CD-ROM. Their task is to create a plan for a 10-minute slot on global Christianity for a Sunday morning TV programme. They should include notes on the visuals they would like to use. For example, what would appear on screen as the prayers are said? The show should include music, prayer and dance. They should explain how each of the items would be introduced, and how each is an expression of both Christian belief and a particular culture.

Gifted and Talented

Explain that Christianity has to maintain a balance between an unchanging message and constantly changing expressions of that message. Ask students to consider what difficulties this presents. Points to think about:

- Can the message be separated from the expression of it?
- The effect of the expression on the message: does the way something is expressed affect the message itself?
- How apt is the saying 'the medium is the message'?

An example they might consider is the argument, put forward by some, that heavy metal music is not an appropriate medium for expressing the Christian message.

Alternatively, students could explore how the Christian message can be expressed in modern western culture without changing the heart of the message. They should give practical examples of how this could be done.

Reflection (All levels)

Music is used to express emotion. Discuss the types of music that people use to express emotion. What do students listen to when they are feeling joyful/fed up/excited? Reflect on why so many people use music to express their feelings.

STIMULUS SHEET 2.7
Prayers from around the world

An African Canticle
by Desmond Tutu

All you big things, bless the Lord.
Mount Kilimanjaro and Lake Victoria,
The Rift Valley and the Serengeti Plain,
Fat baobabs and shady mango trees,
All eucalyptus and tamarind trees,
Bless the Lord.
Praise and extol Him for ever and ever.

All you tiny things, bless the Lord.
Busy black ants and hopping fleas,
Wriggling tadpoles and mosquito larvae,
Flying locusts and water drops,
Pollen dust and tsetse flies,
Millet seeds and dried Dagaa
Bless the Lord.
Praise and extol Him for ever and ever.

Prayer of a Chinese Christian

Heavenly Parent, as the miry bottom of the pond helps the lotus flower to grow, so may our often unlovely environment encourage growth in us. And as the lotus blossom in all its radiance rises above the mire, so help us to transcend our earthly environment to become personalities worthy to be called your children.

An Islander's Prayer from Melanesia
(Pacific Islands)

O Jesus,
Be the canoe that holds me up in the sea of life;
Be the rudder that keeps me in the straight road;
Be the outrigger that supports me in times of temptation.
Let your Spirit be my sail that carries me through each day.
Keep my body strong, so I can paddle steadfastly on in the voyage of life. Amen.

A prayer from Ghana

Years ago our Elders said,
'It is God who drives away flies from the tail-less animal.'
The same God touches each of us with the Spirit of power
To cope and overcome,
To drive away fears and anxieties,
To help us to walk through life in the fire of faith.

Starting the new day
by Masao Takenaka, Japan

Eternal God,
we say good morning to you;
hallowed be your name.
Early in the morning, before we begin our work
We praise your glory.
Renew our bodies as fresh as the morning flowers.
Open our inner eyes, as the sun casts new light upon the darkness
Which prevailed over the night.
Deliver us from all captivity.
Give us wings of freedom like the birds in the sky,
To begin our new journey.
Restore justice and freedom, as a mighty stream
Running continuously as day follows day.
We thank you for the gift of this morning,
And a new day to work with you.

Prayer of the Ojibway nation of Canada
(One of the first nation or Indian peoples)

Grandfather,
Look at our brokenness.
We know that in all creation
Only the human family
Has strayed away from the sacred way.
We know that we are the ones
Who are divided,
And we are the ones who must come back together
To walk in the sacred way.
Grandfather, sacred one,
Teach us love and compassion and honour
That we may heal the earth
And heal each other.

Prayer on a church wall in Mexico

Give us, el Señor, a little sun, a little happiness and some work.
Give us a heart to comfort those in pain.
Give us the ability to be good, strong, wise and free
So that we may be generous with others as we are with ourselves.
Finally, Señor, let us all live in your own, one family.

STIMULUS SHEET 2.8
Songs from around the world

Imela

This is a song of thanksgiving from Nigeria.

Imela imela, imela Okaka.
Imela, Chineke. Imela Ony'oma.

We thank you, thank you Lord,
We thank you, our great God.
We thank you, gracious Lord,
We thank you, our great God.

Santo

This song from Argentina grew out of a people's suffering. It is a heartfelt song expressing love towards God.

Santo, santo, santo,
Mi corazon te adora!
Mi corazon te sabe decir:
Santo eres Señor.

Holy, holy, holy,
My heart, my heart adores you!
My heart is glad to say the words:
You are holy, Lord.

Jesuve Saranam (Jesus, I surrender)

The churches in north and south India have been developing forms of worship and song which relate to their cultural roots. This is a 'call-response' song that is used to call people to worship. (One person sings one part and it is echoed by the people.)

Jesuve saranam,
saranam jesuve (repeated)

Jesus, I surrender.

Many and Great

This song is from the indigenous American community and was published in 1916 in the *Dakota Indian Hymnal*.

Many and Great, O God, are your works,
Maker of Earth and Sky;
Your hands have set the heavens with stars;
Your fingers spread the mountains and plains.
You merely spoke and waters were formed;
Deep seas obey your voice.

Wa Wa Wa Emimimo

This Yoruba song from Nigeria is sung throughout Central Africa.

Wa Wa Wa Emimimo
Wa Wa Wa Alagbara
Wao Wao Wao

Come, O Holy Spirit, come.
Come, Almighty Holy Spirit, come.
Come, come, come.

Recordings of these songs are on the CD-ROM.

Theme 3: **Christianity spreads**

THEME OVERVIEW *This material introduces students to the idea that Christianity is a missionary religion by its very nature and to some of the issues raised by Christian missionary work. Central to Christian faith is the idea that the 'good news' about Jesus is for the whole world. Missionaries are people who take on the task of spreading the Christian message. The subject of Christian mission raises all sorts of questions. Two are particularly important: (1) Why do Christians want to share their beliefs with other people? (2) What right have they to try to change the beliefs and behaviour of others? This theme explores these questions by looking at the issue of truth and its relationship to facts and beliefs. It then examines the way missionary work has changed over the last two hundred years and challenges some of the stereotypes. It also asks students to reflect on their own feelings about the right of people to share their faith with others who hold beliefs different from their own.*

The material provided is:

Option 1: Telling the truth

Option 2: Missionaries, messages and stereotypes

Option 3: The changing role of the missionary

LEARNING OUTCOMES

It is expected that, through using this material, students will:

- think about truth and how one can know what is true (Option 1);

- understand what motivates Christians to share their faith with others (Options 1, 2 and 3);

- question common stereotypes of missionaries (Options 2 and 3);

- learn something about modern Christian missionary work (Options 1, 2 and 3);

- reflect on their own reaction to people wanting to share their beliefs with them (Option 1);

- be able to give reasons for and against evangelism and to express their own opinions on the subject (Option 1).

GLOSSARY

Call of God Religious vocation – a feeling or conviction that you have been chosen by God for special work.

Evangelism Spreading the Christian message (literally the 'evangel' or 'gospel', which means 'good news') so that others may become Christians.

Evangelistic An emphasis on the importance of spreading the Christian message to others.

Gospel The Christian message or 'good news' about Jesus.

Heathen A term widely used until the late nineteenth century to describe people living in non-Christian lands.

Missionary Someone sent by the Church to spread the Christian message by word and action in another place. Those sent overseas from the Church in the West are now often called 'Mission Partners'.

Stereotype A fixed idea considered to represent a particular kind of person. The most common stereotypes are racial, but there are many others, such as religious and sexual.

Option 1: **Telling the truth**

SUMMARY

Why do some people want to share their faith with others? Many people today find the idea of sharing religious beliefs hard to accept. It raises questions like: Shouldn't people be left to work out their own ideas about God? Is it really possible to be sure that you know the truth about God? Does anyone have the right to tell others to change their own beliefs and behaviour? How do I react to people wanting to share their beliefs with me? This material addresses some of these issues and looks at what motivates Christians to share their faith with others.

LEARNING OUTCOMES

It is expected that, through using this material, students will:

- think about truth and how one can know what is true;
- understand what motivates Christians to share their faith with others;
- learn something about modern Christian missionary work;
- reflect on their own reaction to people wanting to share their beliefs with them;
- be able to give reasons for and against evangelism and to express their own opinions on the subject.

RESOURCES REQUIRED

- Stimulus Sheet 3.1: Fact or belief? (1 between two, introduction; the sheets should be cut up so that each group has a set of cards)

- Stimulus Sheet 3.2: Sharing what is important (1 between two, introduction)

- Stimulus Sheet 3.3: The missionary past and present (1 between two, main activity/student tasks)

- Stimulus Sheet 3.4: Sharing the message (optional)

- Recording of the hymn 'The Missionary', sung on CD-ROM (main activity/student tasks)

EXTRA RESOURCES AVAILABLE ON CD-ROM

- Comments on the hymn 'The Missionary' by a modern mission partner

- Pictures of nineteenth-century missionaries

- Recording of the song 'I, the Lord of sea and sky'

TEACHING STEPS

INTRODUCTORY DISCUSSION

1. Ask students to describe the difference between a fact and a belief. Explore the idea that, in popular usage, facts are normally thought to be things that everyone accepts as true whereas beliefs are thought to be a matter of personal preference. Facts, thought of in this way, are often seen as indisputable, whereas beliefs are not.

2. Organize the class into pairs and give each pair a set of the 'Fact or Belief' cards (Sheet 3.1). Ask them to look at each statement and decide whether they think it is a fact or a belief.

(**Note** They are not being asked to say whether the statements are true or false, but whether they appear to be facts or beliefs.) They should sort the cards into two piles – facts and beliefs. The cards should be kept for use in a follow-up discussion. Compare findings.

3. Explain that it may not be as easy as is sometimes assumed to distinguish between facts and beliefs. For example, until as late as the early seventeenth century it was an accepted 'fact' that the sun moved round the earth. The idea that, on the contrary, it was the earth that moved round the sun, first advanced as a theory by Copernicus in the early sixteenth century, was greeted with considerable hostility. Yet it eventually became an accepted 'fact'.

Conclude the discussion by suggesting that facts are things which most people think are true, whereas beliefs are things about which there may be disagreement. In the popular view, facts are true because everyone believes them but beliefs are controversial and probably not true (hence the statement 'That is only your belief'). However, sometimes a 'belief' (such as that the earth travels round the sun) can become a 'fact' as more people accept it. (In the light of this, students may wish to explore different ways of defining a fact.)

4. Now ask the class to repeat the exercise with the cards, but this time to divide their two piles into two different groups – those that really matter and those which, even though they may be true, are not very important. What they will discover is that, contrary to what they might expect, the things that are really important may be beliefs, not facts. The beliefs we hold can be of considerable significance.

5. Hand out Stimulus Sheet 3.2 and ask students to complete the task.

6. As a class, share findings. Conclude the discussion by pointing out that some beliefs are of such significance that the people who hold them believe they are justified in trying to persuade others of their truth. However, the means used is still open to debate. Teachers may wish to refer to Stimulus Sheet 3.4.

MAIN ACTIVITY

1. Give each pair of students a copy of Stimulus Sheet 3.3.

2. Students should follow the words of the hymn as they listen to the recording by Jonathan Kim on the CD-ROM.

3. As a class, discuss the images of missionaries portrayed in the hymn. Focus particularly on the beliefs that have motivated Christians to become missionaries. Comments by a modern mission partner can be found on the CD-ROM.

4. Allocate student tasks.

STUDENT TASKS

Level 3–4 Task
(standard achievement age 11)

Students should consider what mental picture a child living in 1845 might have of a missionary as a result of singing the hymn 'The Missionary'. (Students can see pictures of nineteenth-century missionaries on the CD-ROM.) They should answer the following questions based on the hymn:

- Why would the child want to be a missionary?
- What part of the Christian message is picked out as important for sharing?
- Why do they think that part was seen as important?

Level 5–6 Task
(standard achievement age 14)

Students should be given the level 3–4 task, then asked to imagine they could travel back in time to 1845 and could speak to a young person who has responded to the challenge of the hymn by deciding to become a missionary. What two key questions would they want to ask and why? How do they feel about the work that the missionary wants to do? Is that person justified in wanting to share his/her beliefs?

Level 7–8 Task
(standard achievement age 16)

Students should read the hymn and locate the key ideas in it. Then they should read the statements by the two missionaries and the mission partner's comments on the CD-ROM. Ask them to respond to the following points:

- Locate the key shift in ideas.
- Locate things that have stayed the same.
- Has the way in which people share their beliefs changed?
- What reasons could be given for these changes and the things that have remained unchanged?
- Suggest how the words of the hymn could be altered to suit a modern audience and modern ideas about Christian mission (see page 54).

Gifted and Talented

Ask students to compare the song 'I, the Lord of Sea and Sky' (on CD-ROM) with 'The Missionary', and also look at the comments by the mission partner. What shift, if any, in Christian thinking about the challenge or the underlying message can be detected? What reasons could be given for this shift?

Reflection (All levels)

Ask students to think about a belief that is important to them. Would they want to share it? How would they share their belief in a way that is appropriate both for the belief and for the people who will receive the message? Ask them to reflect on how they feel about other people who want to share their beliefs with them.

STIMULUS SHEET 3.1
Fact or belief?

Note to teachers

The following statements should be photocopied on to card and cut up to provide one set of 'Fact or belief' cards for each pair. Students have to decide whether each statement is a fact or a belief.

There is one God who created the world.	The best things in life are free.	Smoking damages your health.	The Caspian Sea is the world's largest lake (371,000 square km).
A cheetah can sprint at 95 km/h.	The Beatles are the best 'pop' group ever.	There is only one way to heaven and that is through Jesus Christ.	By the end of the 21st century every home in Britain will have access to a computer.
More than half the homes in Iceland are heated by hot volcanic rocks to keep warm.	The rocks in the Grand Canyon date back 500 million years.	A good education gives a child the best start in life.	Lake Pontchartain Causeway in Louisiana, USA, at 38.4 km, is the longest multi-span bridge in the world.
Lima is the capital city of Peru.	Jesus is the Son of God.	Ancient Greeks chewed mastic gum or mastiche to clean their teeth and sweeten their breath.	It doesn't matter what you believe as long as you believe something.
There's no harm in taking drugs as long as you don't let things get out of control.	Watching too much TV dulls the brain.	Jesus said: 'I am the way the truth and the life.'	There's only one thing in life you can be sure about and that is that we are all going to die.
People believe in God because they cannot cope with life as it really is.	Science can explain how things are the way they are and therefore makes God unnecessary.	Manchester United is the best football team in the world at the moment.	Everyone believes something.

STIMULUS SHEET 3.2
Sharing what is important

Look at the six statements below. Do not debate the truth or falsity of the views expressed. What you are required to do, for each one, is:

(a) Decide whether or not it would be appropriate to try to persuade other people of the truth of the statement.

(b) If you judge that it would be appropriate to do so, decide which of the following methods of persuasion would be legitimate:

- talk to your friends
- write letters to newspapers
- organize a political campaign
- take direct action (e.g. by destroying GM crops)

People should reduce the amount of petrol they use in order to conserve fossil fuels and reduce carbon-dioxide pollution.

People should not be allowed to smoke in public places.

Genetically modified food should be banned until there is clear scientific proof that it is safe.

Manchester United is the best football team ever.

Everyone should become vegetarian both for the sake of their own health and to avoid exploiting animals.

People need to know about God for their spiritual well-being.

STIMULUS SHEET 3.3
The missionary: past and present

The hymn on the right is taken from *The Juvenile Missionary Magazine* (November 1845), a Christian publication for children. It illustrates the kind of image children in early Victorian England would have had of missionaries.

Two Modern Missionaries

Kate and Simon Harry, two school teachers from Worcester, went to Nepal with BMS World Mission in 1999. This interview is taken from the Society's magazine for November/December 2000.

Q. *What were you doing five years ago?*

A. *Leading very normal lives. We were busy with friends, setting up a home, church responsibilities and were both enjoying our teaching jobs.*

Q. *What are you doing now?*

A. *We have just completed our first term with BMS World Mission in Nepal. We have been living in a remote Nepali village with no electricity, phone, plumbing or other foreigners nearby. We have been working in the local primary schools training teachers and trying to do anything we can to improve the quality of education.*

Q. *What brought the change about?*

A. *The change came to us as a niggling doubt that turned into a more concrete feeling that we wanted to 'do something' with our lives. God spoke to us through this feeling: he 'unsettled' us and gave us a push.*

'The Missionary'

I'd be a missionary; yes I would labour,
The gospel of Christ I'd to sinners proclaim;
In far distant lands I would tell of a saviour,
Where error and darkness and ignorance reign.
I'd cross the ocean; billows would bear me;
Winds, ye would waft me far over the sea.
I'd be a missionary; heathens would hear me
Proclaim the glad tidings, that "mercy is free!"

Q. *What was the single most important factor in the change?*

A. *We felt we didn't want to get to 50 and wish that we had taken more risks and trusted God more, rather than getting stuck in a suburban rut.*

Q. *How would you say God is working through what you're doing?*

A. *People are open to talk about different beliefs and we've had some promising conversations. The people are also aware that we treat each other differently, that men and women are equal and that marriage is a partnership. We also hope that Christian values such as truth and honesty, equality and love have been shown through the work there. There are glimmers of hope in the classrooms too, and children are getting a much better deal at school.*

STIMULUS SHEET 3.4
Sharing the message

Christians believe that the Christian message is good news (the meaning of the word 'gospel'). That is why many of them want to share their beliefs. Below are some comments from Christians about sharing their faith.

Many people feel alone and I would want to say that God is with us always. We are never alone.

A church member

God our Creator loves us so much that he sent his Son to share our life and lead us to eternal happiness.

A Roman Catholic nun

Christianity is a message worth sharing with everyone because Jesus Christ offers a world that is out of joint the only hope of being put together again as God intended.

A writer

Jesus became one of us and knows exactly what we face in life.

A teacher

I would want to say that people can have a personal relationship with God.

A missionary

Option 2: **Missionaries, messages and stereotypes**

SUMMARY

Missionaries are people who are passionate about sharing their beliefs with other people. This is because they are sure these beliefs are vitally important and have profound implications for everyone. This material illustrates these ideas through a study of the life of Samuel Crowther, an African who became a missionary. This example also helps to dispel the misconception that only white people were missionaries.

LEARNING OUTCOMES

It is expected that, through using this material, students will:

- understand what motivates Christians to share their faith with others;

- question common stereotypes of missionaries;

- learn something about modern Christian missionary work.

RESOURCES REQUIRED

- Stimulus Sheet 3.5: missionary pictures (1 between two, introduction)

- Stimulus Sheet 3.6: cartoon strip story of Samuel Crowther (1 between two, student tasks)

- Stimulus Sheet 3.7: What do Christians believe? (1 between two, student tasks)

- Stimulus Sheet 3.8: Missionaries and colonialism (student task, gifted and talented only)

- Map of Africa showing Sierra Leone/Freetown, on CD-ROM (OHT)

EXTRA RESOURCES AVAILABLE ON CD-ROM

- Pictures of the missionary stereotype and modern pictures of missionaries

- Picture of Samuel Crowther and more information about him

- Map of Africa showing Sierra Leone

- Information sheet on how Christianity came to West Africa (background information for teachers)

TEACHING STEPS

INTRODUCTORY DISCUSSION

1. Explain that missionaries are Christians who believe that the message of Jesus is so important they want to tell other people about it. See Stimulus Sheet 3.7.

2. Discuss what images the word 'missionary' conjures up. Do the pictures on Stimulus Sheet 3.5 match these images? (An extra picture can be found on the CD-ROM.) Brainstorm all the implicit messages that are associated with pictures like this (white superiority, forcing people to adopt European culture, depicting native people as 'primitive' or 'heathen', etc.). At the end of this session go back to the picture and ask pupils if their image of a missionary has changed.

3. Using the map, find Sierra Leone and Freetown. Explain that Sierra Leone was set up as a safe haven for slaves freed by the British Navy when they intercepted the slave traders' ships. That is why its capital is called Freetown. This gives the necessary background to the life of Samuel Crowther, who is an unusual missionary in that he doesn't fit most people's preconceived ideas. He was an African who worked as a missionary among other Africans. Background information for teachers about how Christianity came to West Africa can be found on the CD-ROM.

MAIN ACTIVITY

1. Hand out Stimulus Sheet 3.6 and ask students to read it. Allocate student tasks.

2. Option: ask students to look back at the photograph of the Lambeth Conference in 1867 (page 25). Samuel Crowther was missing from

this conference. Ask students to suggest reasons why he was not present. How do they think people might have felt about a black bishop, bearing in mind that he was the first to be appointed by the Anglican Church?

STUDENT TASKS

Level 3–4 Task

(standard achievement age 11)

Ask students to look at the pictures of the nineteenth-century missionaries on Stimulus Sheet 3.5. Can they suggest in what ways did Samuel Crowther not fulfil these stereotypes? They should make a list of the risks he took. What part of the Christian message (Sheet 3.7) do they think Samuel Crowther believed was so important that he was prepared to risk his life? See the CD-ROM for pictures of Crowther, a missionary and a map.

Level 5–6 Task

(standard achievement age 14)

Ask students to imagine that they are doing the research for a chat show (such as 'Parkinson'). They should use the CD-ROM to find out more about Samuel Crowther and then create a list of questions to ask that will probe his motives as a missionary and the reasons why he took the risks he did. Now they should change the situation to a more aggressive journalistic (Paxman-type) interview. How would the questions differ? The questions can become the basis for student discussion or role-play.

Level 7–8 Task

(standard achievement age 16)

Ask students to read Stimulus Sheet 3.7. What do they think Samuel Crowther would have wanted to share first? What would have been lower on the list? They should give reasons for their answers.

Missionaries are stereotyped as being white and western almost by definition (see the pictures on the CD-ROM), and Christianity is often seen as a mainly white, western faith. This is not true to history. Christianity started in the Middle East and for many years North Africa was a Christian stronghold. One of Christianity's greatest thinkers, St Augustine of Hippo, came from Africa. Ask students to consider whether it alters the way we think of missionaries if we view Christianity as a non-western religion. They should imagine that Christianity has just been attacked in a local paper as a white, western faith and write a reply drawing on the stimulus sheets and material on the CD-ROM.

Gifted and Talented

Explain that missionaries are sometimes seen as the spiritual arm of western capitalism. Some people thought that slaves and subject people (the 'natives' and the 'heathen') were taught the Christian faith in order to make them submissive. Yet missionaries were often opposed by traders and those in government. Teaching slaves to read the Bible was also seen as subversive as it encouraged them to think for themselves.

Students should read Stimulus Sheet 3.8 and then write down why they think certain groups opposed the spreading of the Christian message. What reasons can be found in the material? Can they suggest reasons that are not being admitted?

Ask them to look at Stimulus Sheet 3.7. Which parts would be thought of as dangerous? Why? Is there any basis for seeing missionaries as dangerous radicals or liberators? Students should justify their answers.

Reflection (All levels)

Ask students to think about older people's stereotypes of 'young people'. What is right about those stereotypes? What is wrong with them? Now ask them to think about common stereotypes of missionaries. Look at the pictures of missionaries again. Discuss what it would take to change people's ideas about missionaries. What is the most effective way to change stereotypes?

STIMULUS SHEET 3.5
Missionary pictures

Two pictures of nineteenth–century missionaries

Sebastian and Kirsteen Kim

Sebastian is a Presbyterian minister from South Korea and his wife, Kirsteen, is a mathematics teacher from England. They have served the Church in western India, helping to train Indian ministers.

Pictures are available on the CD-ROM.

STIMULUS SHEET 3.6
The story of Samuel Crowther

In 1807 Britain passed a law abolishing the slave trade.

British naval squadrons based in Sierra Leone began intercepting slave ships from other countries and freeing the slaves.

A large colony of freed slaves grew up in Sierra Leone. Their capital was named 'Freetown'.

Ajayi came from the town of Osogun in Yorubaland, which is now Western Nigeria.

One day he was captured by slave traders and led away with a rope around his neck. He was to be taken to America as a slave.

Ajayi was to be shipped across the Atlantic by Portuguese traders, but he was rescued by the British Navy and taken to Sierre Leone.

Ajayi was taken to Freetown. He became a Christian and was baptized by a British missionary in 1825. He was given the English name Samuel Crowther.

He became one of the first students at Fourah Bay College and went on to teach freed African slaves and their children.

Ajayi may have been back in Africa, but he was a thousand miles from his home. He wanted to share the Christian message with his own people.

He led a mission to Yorubaland, his home country. Forty-two members of his party died and the mission was abandoned.

In 1857 he led another mission, along the Niger River, where, after 25 years, he was reunited with his mother. In 1864 he was appointed the first black Anglican bishop.

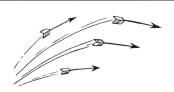

On one mission, an African chief, who was angry with the British traders, kidnapped Samuel and his son. They escaped, but had to flee as they were shot at with poisoned arrows.

What do Christians believe?

Below are *some* of the things that
Christians believe:

God is Father, Son and Holy Spirit.

God made the world and made us to live in friendship with him but we turned against him and wrecked that friendship.

Jesus is God's son, God himself, who came to live among us as a human being. He knows what our lives are like.

By the life, death and resurrection of Jesus Christ God has dealt with all that separates us from him, and brought us back into friendship with him.

After Jesus returned to his Father, he sent the Holy Spirit (God invisible but active) who is with us always.

People can learn more about God from the Bible, which God uses to speak to his people, the Church.

People communicate with God through prayer and worship.

One day all men and women will have to answer to God for what they have done with their lives.

As children of God all Christians are brothers and sisters – members of a global family called the Church.

STIMULUS SHEET 3.8
Missionaries and colonialism

Missionaries are often seen as the religious arm of empire, but as early as the sixteenth century, Jesuit missionaries fought for the rights of South American peoples as the Spanish Empire expanded.

Very few missionaries in the nineteenth and early twentieth centuries opposed the western colonial empires on principle (hardly anybody in the West at that time believed that empire was wrong). However, missionaries made themselves unpopular with colonial authorities and white settlers as a result of their preaching and consistent defence of the interests of the indigenous people.

Far from missionaries being an arm of the colonial administration, in India they were originally prohibited by the East India Company from entering their territory without a licence, something which was often hard to obtain. (The East India Company administered British India until 1858.) The first British missionaries, such as William Carey, broke the rules by entering company territory without a licence. Their presence alarmed the company authorities, who feared that their activities would upset the indigenous population and injure the company's profits.

The early missionaries were of humble social origins and were regarded with contempt by the respectable portions of society. Sydney Smith, the essayist, wrote a famous attack on the British missionaries in India in 1808. In this he sneered:

'Why are we to send out little detachments of maniacs to spread over the fine regions of the world the most unjust and contemptible opinion of the gospel? The wise and rational part of the Christian ministry find they have enough to do at home to combat with passions unfavourable to human happiness, and to make men act up to their professions. But if a tinker is a devout man, he infallibly sets off for the East.'

In the West Indies, missionaries made themselves unpopular with the colonial authorities by their defence of the interests of slaves against their masters. The Jamaican House of Assembly (parliament) adopted a report in 1828 that decried missionaries and alleged that:

'… to gain an ascendancy over the Negro mind they inculcate the doctrines of equality and the rights of man.'

The slave-owners were right to be worried. Within five years, missionaries and their supporters in Britain had successfully worked for an end to slavery in the British colonies. The missionaries and Jamaican Christians who led the campaign for freedom of the slaves are remembered with great respect in Jamaica today.

Missionaries in the twentieth century maintained this tradition of standing up for the rights of indigenous people. In Kenya in the 1920s, Archdeacon W. E. Owen, a missionary who defended the land rights of the local people, was so hated by the British settlers that he was given the nickname 'Archdemon Owen'.

Option 3: The changing role of the missionary

SUMMARY

There have been dramatic changes in Christian understanding of the missionary's role since the nineteenth century. Missionary work is no longer seen as a 'one-way street', with missionaries coming from the 'civilized' Christian world and taking their message to the 'primitive and heathen' developing world. Rather, it is seen as more of a partnership between people from different cultures. So today, people from Africa, Asia, the Far East and all over the globe travel the world and even come to Britain to work with churches. (See Stimulus Sheet 3.4 and the pictures of missionaries on the CD-ROM.)

LEARNING OUTCOMES

It is expected that, through using this material, students will:

- understand what motivates Christians to share their faith with others;

- question common stereotypes of missionaries;

- learn something about modern Christian missionary work.

RESOURCES REQUIRED

- Stimulus Sheet 3.9: Missionaries today (1 for the teacher, main activity)

- Stimulus Sheet 3.10: Requirements for mission partners (either OHT or 1 between two, main activity, student tasks)

- Stimulus Sheet 3.11: Job file (either OHT or 1 between two, student tasks)

- Material on Samuel Azariah (CD-ROM, level 7–8 only)

- List of mission agencies (CD-ROM, gifted and talented only)

EXTRA RESOURCES AVAILABLE ON CD-ROM

- Case studies – Mission partners around the world

- How missionary societies began

- A missionary link letter

- Material on Samuel Azariah

- List of mission agencies

TEACHING STEPS

INTRODUCTORY DISCUSSION

1. Read out the advertisement below or cut out some 'Situations vacant' adverts from a newspaper that include the requirement for a 'team-worker' as part of the job. Discuss what the term 'team-worker' means and ask students to suggest two difficulties and two advantages of working as part of a team.

   Leader required for a team of workers on a community project in Kenya. Must have previous experience of leading and working in teams, be able to work alongside people from a variety of backgrounds and to co-operate with other team leaders on this project.

2. Discuss reasons why the ability to work in a team is considered so important in many jobs today.

3. Ask students to consider what they would reply if they were asked at a job interview what they were like as team-workers. (Students should think about this: their thoughts do not have to be shared.)

MAIN ACTIVITY

1. Display the following list of statements on the board or OHP and ask students to vote 'true' or 'false' on each.

   - There used to be lots of Christian missionaries but there aren't so many today.

   - There are more missionaries now than 100 years ago.

   - Missionaries come from the western world and work in the third world.

   - Missionaries come to work in Britain from places such as Africa.

- Missionaries only do 'religious' jobs, such as telling people about Jesus.

- Missionaries work independently of the local Christians.

- Most missionaries are men.

2. Read out a selection of information from Stimulus Sheet 3.9. Does this change any of the students' answers? Display the questions at the foot of the sheet and ask students to write answers to them.

3. Explain that when the modern missionary movement began, people were sent from Europe and North America to other parts of the world (see 'How missionary societies began' on the CD-ROM). Now, however, mission involves the movement of people in many different directions. (See 'Case Studies – Mission partners around the world' on the CD-ROM.)

4. Either hand out or display Stimulus Sheet 3.10 on OHT. Ask students to look for the 'clues' in the text as evidence that missionary work has changed to one of partnership.

5. Allocate student tasks.

STUDENT TASKS

Level 3–4 Task

(standard achievement age 11)

Ask students to look at the list of requirements on Stimulus Sheet 3.10. Which one (excluding the last) do they think the mission society would regard as the most important? Why?

Ask students to choose one job from Stimulus Sheet 3.11 and imagine working in that situation. They should write a diary entry for one day that illustrates how they work in partnership with local people.

Level 5–6 Task

(standard achievement age 14)

Using Stimulus Sheet 3.10, students should list the requirements in order of importance (a) from the point of view of the mission agency they will be working for, and (b) from the point of view of the people they will be serving. They should justify their decision. Which point do they think is the most important quality for a missionary?

Ask students to choose one job from Stimulus Sheet 3.11 and imagine working in that situation. They should write a diary entry for one day that illustrates how there may be difficulties in working in partnership with local people – for example, in the education or health care of girls.

Level 7–8 Task

(standard achievement age 16)

Ask students to look at the requirements on Stimulus Sheet 3.10 and divide them into three categories: personal qualities, professional skills and religious commitment. Which of these three categories are most important for working in partnership? Why?

Ask students to look at the article on Samuel Azariah on the CD-ROM. Using the highlighting/underlining facility, they should mark sections that illustrate his desire for partnership. (Alternatively, they can print out and highlight.) Ask them to consider in what ways Samuel Azariah's hopes have been fulfilled in the changes in the requirements for mission partners.

Gifted and Talented

Suggest that students look at the missionary links letter on the CD-ROM. Ask them to devise a series of questions that probe the issues this practice raises. They should define any problems that they think missionaries to this country might meet.

Some mission agencies now advertise posts via the Internet. For example, visit the CWM website (The Council for World Mission, which is descended from the former London Missionary Society), on **www.cwmission.org.uk/activities/vacs.htm**. This shows the latest 'Missionary Vacancies' list, which may make an interesting resource to explore. The main headings indicate the type of jobs on offer in a variety of countries.

Reflection (All levels)

Explain that partnership works because people bring different but complementary contributions. Ask students to design a symbol that captures the meaning of the word 'partnership'. As they do so, they should reflect on times when they have achieved things by working in partnership with other people. They should think about the particular contributions they brought, and the contributions of other people that complemented their own.

Missionaries today

True or false?

Some people think that missionaries died out with the end of the British Empire, but the truth is that there are more missionaries now than ever before. It is estimated that there are some 420,000 missionaries (men and women) in the world today, compared with 62,000 in 1900. But there have been changes in the way missionaries work and the kind of jobs they do.

The Church Mission (formerly Missionary) Society, for example, has changed the name it gives to its missionaries. It now calls them 'mission partners'. This reflects the fact that these missionaries work in partnership with and at the invitation of the churches in the country where they will work.

"DEAR MUM.... BEING A MISSIONARY ISN'T QUITE WHAT I THOUGHT IT WOULD BE...."

© Cartoon by Michael Henesy. © Kevin Mayhew Ltd. Used by permission – from *Instant Art for the Church Magazine*. Licence no.103091.

THE FACTS

- **In 1999 CMS had about 165 mission partners working around the world.**

- **Christians from the western world still go as missionaries to other countries. In 1999 The Catholic Missionary Union had 506 missionaries from England and Wales working overseas.**

- **Mission partners train new Christian leaders, help with community development projects, work with refugee groups, teach, provide medical help and share their faith.**

- **Other countries also send people to work alongside Christians in Britain. Many Christians recognize that the Church in Britain, like other western countries, is in need of help from their Christian partners in places like Africa and Asia.**

- **Some people are surprised that countries that used to be thought of as 'mission fields' are now sending missionaries or mission partners to Britain.**

- **The move to 'mission partners' signalled some important changes in the way missionaries are selected and the type of work that they do. Many are expected to combine professional skills with Christian commitment and the challenge of serving God with a local church in a different culture.**

- **Most CMS mission partners work under the authority of local church leaders.**

Two questions to consider:

1. Why do you think CMS no longer uses the term 'missionaries'?

2. Why do you think that some people are surprised, even alarmed, that the churches now invite Christians from other countries to come to Britain to work?

Requirements for mission partners

People selected by CMS must fulfil the following requirements to be considered as mission partners.

They must be:

- **actively involved in their local church;**

- **growing in their faith;**

- **sensitive to God's calling to service in a different culture;**

- **able to see that God is present and at work in cultures different from their own;**

- **capable of working harmoniously with Christian traditions that are different from their own;**

- **suitably qualified to meet the needs of partner churches;**

- **able to meet the visa and work-permit requirements of the host countries.**

CMS usually has openings for development workers, theological educators, clergy, teachers of English as a foreign language and other subjects, doctors, nurses and other health professionals.

STIMULUS SHEET 3.11
Job file

SOLOMON ISLANDS

Two graduate teachers required to teach science and English, particularly for sixth-form classes at Goldie College. This is a secondary boarding school with 4000 students, administered by the church.

PAPUA NEW GUINEA

A lawyer for work on church land and property is required for one year, based in Port Moresby.

SAMOA

Secondary school teachers of biology, chemistry, physics and English are needed.

BANGLADESH

A general surgeon is needed, either long term or short term, to work at a Christian Mission hospital in Rajshahi.

PAPUA NEW GUINEA

A mission-enabler is needed for two years to empower local congregations. (A mission-enabler is someone who gives others the skills they need to do their own mission work.)

ZAMBIA

The United Church in Zambia needs a financial secretary to serve for two years. Based in the church in Lusaka.

BOTSWANA

Medical officer/nurse needed for Moeding College, a school with 1600 students. Botswana is rated first among all countries affected by HIV/AIDS. It is estimated that 25% of all young people are HIV positive.

PAPUA NEW GUINEA

Industrial chaplains required for a number of two-year placements, mainly in multi-racial, multi-cultural mining communities.

Theme 4: Changing faith

THEME OVERVIEW *The subject of religious conversion is a controversial one. But it cannot be ignored in any serious study of religion, since it is such an important element of the Christian experience of life. This theme seeks to tackle this potentially sensitive issue through the eyes of people who have converted, using stories, personal experiences, interviews and case studies as a basis for further exploration.*

The material covered raises a number of questions. What causes people to change their faith? Is conversion simply an individual decision? Does conversion mean totally abandoning one's previous faith? To what degree does a change of faith mean a change of culture? How do the people closest to someone react to them after a religious conversion? The material illustrates that most conversions involve the convert in a creative integration of their former and new experience and beliefs, so that they become what has been called 'a skilled cultural navigator'. It also challenges students to think about the legitimacy of seeking religious conversions and gives them the opportunity to reflect on their own reaction to people wanting to persuade them to change their ideas or beliefs.

The material provided is:

Option 1: What leads people to change their faith?

Option 2: Following the tribe?

Option 3: Facing persecution

LEARNING OUTCOMES

It is expected that, through using this material, students will:

- reflect on what causes people to change their faith (Options 1, 2 and 3);

- assess the degree to which conversion changes a person's way of life or culture (Option 1);

- reflect on the impact of change in their own lives (Option 1);

- understand the concept of group conversion and consider its validity (Option 2);

- reflect on the influence of peer pressure (Option 2);

- be able to explain why changing religion can cause controversy and bring persecution (Options 2 and 3).

GLOSSARY

Caste system A hierarchical pattern of social organization which exists in India. All Indian people are born into a caste associated traditionally with a particular occupation. There are four main groups of castes. At the top of the hierarchy are the Brahmins or priests. Next come those who were traditionally soldiers or people in positions of leadership. They are followed by the shopkeepers, traders and farmers. The lowest of the four are the servant castes. Below them are the 'outcastes' or 'untouchables', known most frequently today as 'Dalits', meaning 'broken' or 'oppressed' people. People are not supposed to marry outside their own caste, and close contact, such as eating, with a member of a lower caste is regarded as polluting. Almost all scholars agree that the caste system remains extremely strong in Hindu communities in India today.

Conversion A fundamental change of direction or allegiance, especially in relation to one's beliefs or faith. In western societies, conversion is usually something that happens to individuals. In other parts of the world, people may convert as groups. A conversion process usually comprises a number of elements or motives – intellectual, moral, spiritual, emotional and material – but the balance between these different ingredients may vary markedly from one instance to another. A conversion that involves only one of these categories is unlikely to be complete or permanent.

Dalit A member of an 'untouchable' caste at the very bottom of India's social hierarchy. These people are regarded as polluting by members of higher castes. The word 'Dalit' means 'crushed' or 'oppressed'.

Karma A Hindu belief concerning the way in which actions in this life affect the experience of the next reincarnation.

Karmic debt A Hindu belief concerning the way in which actions in this life can build up a debt to be paid in another.

Konars A higher-caste group in the Puliyur area.

Paraiyars A large Dalit caste of agricultural labourers in southern India.

Persecution Heavy oppression of a person or of many people.

Reconciliation Sorting out current or past problems and getting back together as friends or partners.

Option 1: **What leads people to change their faith?**

SUMMARY

This material concentrates on what it means to convert from one faith (in this case Hinduism) to another (Christianity). Conversion from Christianity to other religions also occurs, of course. The material examines what causes people to convert and the kinds of changes that this brings about in their lives. The material raises questions concerning the connections between faith, culture and religious practices. It emphasizes the fact that conversion is rarely a total abandoning of a person's old way of life, but is rather a redefining and refocusing of their understanding of the various influences on them. Finally, the material invites students to reflect on significant changes in their own lives, challenging them to consider the impact such experiences have.

LEARNING OUTCOMES

It is expected that, through using this material, students will:

- reflect on what causes people to change their faith;
- assess the degree to which conversion changes a person's way of life or culture;
- reflect on the impact of change in their own lives.

RESOURCES REQUIRED

- Stimulus Sheet 4.1: The story of Pandita Ramabai (1 between two, main activity/student tasks)
- Stimulus Sheet 4.2: Extract from interview with Ram Gidoomal (1 between two, main activity/student tasks)
- Extra material on Pandita Ramabai and Ram Gidoomal on CD-ROM (Levels 7–8 only)

EXTRA RESOURCES AVAILABLE ON CD-ROM

- Extra material on Pandita Ramabai and Ram Gidoomal (including the full text of the interview with Janet King)
- Photograph of Ram Gidoomal

TEACHING STEPS

INTRODUCTORY DISCUSSION

1. Discuss how someone might become a convert to vegetarianism after witnessing the treatment of turkeys at a local turkey farm. Ask students for other examples of these types of 'conversions'.

2. Brainstorm the word 'conversion'. Look at the results. Discuss whether these words apply to both religious and non-religious conversions.

3. Look at the words/phrases that students think apply to religious conversion. Discuss the meaning of the word 'conversion' in a religious context. Consider what it means to experience conversion. (**Note** This section looks at conversion from Hinduism to Christianity. Students may wish to explore other conversions, e.g. from Christianity to Buddhism.)

4. Divide the words/phrases that apply to religious conversion into positive and negative statements. (For example, 'leaving the religion you were brought up in' is a negative statement, but 'finding a new faith' is a positive one.) Using some words from both groups, write a class definition of 'conversion' on the board.

MAIN ACTIVITY

1. Using Stimulus Sheet 4.1, read through the important events in Pandita Ramabai's life. Discuss the significance of these events. Alternatively, using Stimulus Sheet 4.2, read through the interview with Ram Gidoomal, picking out the important points and discussing them.

2. Allocate student tasks. Afterwards bring the class together to share their findings. Make sure they understand what things influence/make it easier for people to convert and the results of conversion.

3. Ask students to think about their own attitudes to 'conversion'. Many people in the West have negative attitudes towards this idea because they associate it with undue pressure and possible loss of community and culture. But it is an issue that involves freedom of speech and freedom of belief. Should we not give people the freedom to change their religion? How will people hear of alternatives if no one tells them? These ideas can be discussed.

STUDENT TASKS

Level 3–4 Task

(standard achievement age 11)

Ask students to identify some of the things that influenced Pandita Ramabai to change her faith (Sheet 4.1). Which influence do they think was the strongest? They should give reasons for their answers. Alternatively, ask them to read the interview with Ram Gidoomal (Sheet 4.2) and write about the way others reacted to his change of faith and how he responded to that reaction.

Level 5–6 Task

(standard achievement age 14)

Use the task above, based on Sheet 4.1, but ask students to divide the influences into internal ones (such as dissatisfaction) and external ones (such as meeting Christians). Alternatively, use the Ram Gidoomal interview and ask students to look for evidence of ways in which his new faith allowed him to remain part of the culture in which he had been brought up. Extra material can be found on the CD-ROM.

Level 7–8 Task

(standard achievement age 16)

Point out to students that both Pandita Ramabai and Ram Gidoomal use the phrase 'Hindu Christians'. Ask students to list ways in which both these people remained Hindu when they became Christian. Ask them to consider how their Christianity might differ from the Christianity of someone brought up in western culture. Extra material can be found on the CD-ROM.

Gifted and Talented

Ask students to read both stimulus sheets and create a summary of the issues involved. They should then create a symbolic representation of conversion. They will need to consider how they can represent the continuity/discontinuity of these experiences. They should write an explanation of their symbol.

Reflection (All levels)

Ask students to think about a 'defining moment' in their lives – this could be an important meeting or conversation with someone or a key event that in some way changed their life or influenced them. In what way did this encounter or incident change them and in what way did it leave them the same? Ask them to spend a few quiet moments considering these points. They may want to share their thoughts with someone or they may prefer to keep them to themselves.

STIMULUS SHEET 4.1
The story of Pandita Ramabai

In 1858 Ramabai is born into a high-caste, devout Hindu family.

Her father was a wandering Hindu guru and a reformer. He taught Ramabai the ancient Sanskrit language.

The family travel around India, visiting Hindu shrines. Unfortunately, Ramabai's parents die.

Ramabai continues visiting shrines and giving lectures on Hinduism for three years, but she becomes increasingly dissatisfied.

In 1878, Ramabai is given a copy of the Bible in Sanskrit.

She is given the honorary title 'Pandita' in recognition of her teaching.

Ramabai studies the Bible, Hindu teaching and philosophy, especially attitudes towards women and the poor.

Ramabai marries a Bengali man from a lower caste. Her husband dies of cholera after only two years of marriage, leaving her to bring up their daughter alone.

In 1883 Ramabai and her daughter visit England and stay with the nuns at the convent of St Mary in Wantage, Oxford.

Ramabai is taken to Fulham to see the work of the nuns in a home for unmarried mothers. She is greatly impressed by their love for and devotion to the women.

A nun explains their Christian motivation for this work through the story of Jesus and the Samaritan woman (John ch. 4).
Ramabai becomes a Christian and is baptised on 29th September 1883.

On returning to India, Ramabai enjoys a high profile, but faces opposition to her teaching of Christianity.

Ramabai is convinced that her acceptance of Christianity had been largely an intellectual one and that she needs a more personal experience of conversion. In her own words she accepts 'her need of Christ and not merely his religion'.

Ramabai sets about her work with a fresh zeal. She opens a home for Hindu widows in 1889 in Bombay.

Although Ramabai continued to study the Bible all her life and put what she learned into practice as a Christian, she never forgot her Hindu roots, calling herself a 'Hindu Christian'. She believed that her new faith did not require her to abandon the cultural heritage that was part of her life.

STIMULUS SHEET 4.2
Extract from interview with Ram Gidoomal

Ram Gidoomal is a successful businessman, writer and politician. He is a Christian who converted from being a Hindu. In May 2000 he stood as a candidate for Mayor of London on behalf of a new political party called the Christian People's Alliance. He didn't win, but he gained 100,000 votes, beating every other minority party.

Janet King

Ram Gidoomal

Janet King: *Most people are probably asking: 'Who is Ram Gidoomal?'*

Ram Gidoomal: My family was expelled from India in 1947 when India was partitioned, so they went to Kenya. History then repeated itself when, in 1967, the family was uprooted again and that's when we came to the UK and started life here as refugees.

Janet: *It must have been hard for you adjusting to a new way of life.*

Ram: Yes, one of the first things I noticed was Christian assemblies at the local school. I soon realized that there were hundreds of years of Christian tradition and heritage in Britain. My family was Hindu.

Janet: *You are a businessman, a writer, an advisor to the Prince's Youth Business Trust, a politician, a family man and a Christian. What is most important to you now?*

Ram: The most important thing to me is the fact that I believe in Jesus.

Janet: *How did your family react to you changing your religion?*

Ram: When I told my mum she was very upset, but my parents did not reject me. They did ask me lots of questions about my faith. I told them that for me, Jesus is the Sanatana Sat Guru, that is the Eternal, True and Living Way, or as Jesus Himself said: 'I am the way, the truth and the life.' John (14 v. 6). Talking about Jesus as the Sanatana Sat Guru has opened up a way for me to talk about my Christian faith in a safe, non-threatening way.

Janet: *Do you think Christianity can be expressed in different cultures?*

Ram: Yes, I believe that the Christian faith can be expressed in many different cultures. In the Asian community, we celebrate Diwali as a festival of lights. So, in some Asian Churches we have a 'Christian Diwali Service' where we celebrate Jesus as The Light of the World and think about how we can be 'lights' in this world.

Janet: *Some people who convert from Hinduism to Christianity call themselves 'Hindu Christians'. What do you feel about this?*

Ram: The term 'Hindu' was coined by the British. For me it refers to a sense of community and origin. In this sense I was, and still am, Hindu, but I choose to call myself a Hindu follower of Jesus Christ. I hope that I am communicating that I am not abandoning my culture

Janet: *Did life change for you when you became a Christian?*

Ram: Yes, but slowly. I started to read the Bible, and to pray to Jesus. Being a follower of Jesus also began to affect my business practices. I realized that it wasn't right to accept goods that had 'fallen off the back of a lorry' and I had to stop stocking and selling pornographic magazines in the shop. My mother thought that becoming a Christian meant that I would now start going to pubs and acting like a white person. But what actually happened was that I began to see the value of respecting one's parents and the value of prayer, etc.

Janet: *You talk about similarities between Hinduism and Christianity. What do you mean by that?*

Ram: In Christianity and Hinduism there is an emphasis on 'doing good'. The Ten Commandments, for example, have many parallels in Hinduism and Sikhism. There are important differences though. As a Christian, I believe that Jesus paid the 'karmic debt' and because of that I can have everlasting life – forever with God.

Option 2: **Following the tribe?**

SUMMARY

This material raises the issue of group conversion, something that is probably quite alien to the individualistic western mind. Students will be asked to consider its validity and to reflect on the importance of having a sense of group identity. A comparison is drawn between the pressure felt by villagers to conform to the group when conversion takes place and the feeling of peer pressure that most students will have experienced at some time in their lives.

LEARNING OUTCOMES

It is expected that, through using this material, students will:

- reflect on what causes people to change their faith;

- understand the concept of group conversion and consider its validity;

- reflect on the influence of peer pressure;

- be able to explain why changing religion can cause controversy and bring persecution.

RESOURCES REQUIRED

- Stimulus Sheet 4.3: An extract from the Nicky Cruz story (1 between two, introduction)

- Stimulus Sheet 4.4: Newspaper article: *The Ramnad News* (1 between two, main activity/student tasks)

- Stimulus Sheet 4.5: 'Every face tells a story' (1 between two, main activity/student tasks)

EXTRA RESOURCES AVAILABLE ON CD-ROM

- Background information on David Wilkerson

- Details of books about Nicky Cruz

- Village conversion in Ramnad

TEACHING STEPS

INTRODUCTORY DISCUSSION

1. Using Stimulus Sheet 4.3, discuss how a whole group of people can be influenced by one person to change their normal pattern of behaviour and take on a different set of values. See CD-ROM for background information.

2. Brainstorm the different groups that the students (or the population at large) belong to, e.g. fan clubs, social groups, activity groups, and so on. Talk about why they belong to these groups. Focus on the idea of having a common identity and purpose and the benefits people gain from being part of a group. How is that identity expressed? When is it helpful to act as a group? (E.g. activity groups where people rely on each other.) When does group identity become a problem? (E.g. hooliganism.) Introduce the notion of peer pressure. When is this positive? When is it negative?

3. Now explain the term 'group conversion' (see glossary) and what it means in a religious context. Discuss why group conversion is not such a common idea in western cultures or societies. What reasons can students suggest for this?

MAIN ACTIVITY

1. Using Stimulus Sheets 4.4 and 4.5, familiarize students with what happened at Puliyur and ask them to complete the task on sheet 4.5. Explain

that Westerners tend to see themselves as individuals first and members of groups/communities second. In Asian communities people often think the other way round. Background information on group conversion can be found on the CD-ROM.

2. Allocate student tasks. Bring the class back together to review their findings and to check that students have grasped the key concept of group conversion and what this means.

3. These are some important questions that can be discussed:

   - Is group conversion legitimate?
   - Is it 'right' to convert to a religion for material or other benefits?
   - What positive things can be learned from the way the villagers of Puliyur acted as a group?
   - What issues/questions does this subject raise?

STUDENT TASKS

Level 3–4 Task

(standard achievement age 11)

Ask students to consider, in the story of Puliyur, who converted as a group and why. What were the benefits of acting as a group rather than as individuals? Students should imagine they are foreign correspondents for a western television programme. How would they report this incident so that a western audience could understand it? Ask them to prepare a script for a two-minute broadcast.

Level 5–6 Task

(standard achievement age 14)

As above, but students should imagine that the broadcast is two-way and listeners are able to e-mail questions. They should consider what might be asked and how they would respond. What do they think might prevent group conversion in the West?

Level 7–8 Task

(standard achievement age 16)

Ask students to role-play a scene in a TV studio where a documentary-drama based on this story is being planned. They should decide on the different characters that would need to be present at the meeting (keep the group small). They should create role-play cards for the drama, and a basic storyboard of the programme that will communicate the idea of group conversion and the motives for it. What issues might be raised in the minds of a western audience?

Gifted and Talented

Students should imagine they have been asked to act as consultant for the TV programme outlined in the Level 7–8 task. What would they advise the programme makers concerning the way they represent the feelings of the communities and not just individuals? For example, using 'vox pop' only reinforces the emphasis on the individual. Is there another way of gathering views?

Students should list sensitive ethical issues raised by the subject matter and say what advice they would give about handling these issues. They should also consider how they would help the audience understand the perspective of the people involved.

Reflection (all levels)

Ask students to think of a group to which they belong. What benefits do they enjoy as a result of belonging to that group? Why did they join? Did they feel under any pressure to join? Would they ever change their membership of a group in order to get more benefits? (An example could be given of a football supporter who, when their current team fail to qualify for a European competition, changes teams in order to follow the new club to Europe.) Students should be asked to respond to this task on an individual basis and there should be no compulsion to share their responses with the rest of the class.

STIMULUS SHEET 4.3
An extract from the Nicky Cruz story

David Wilkerson felt he was called to spread the Christian message to teenagers caught up in the gang culture of New York. See the CD–ROM for more information.

David's idea of hiring a theatre and inviting the rival gangs to a Christian meeting did not seem such a good one now! All the gangs were there except the Mau Maus. Suddenly, the doors were flung open and 50 Mau Mau marched in, headed by Israel and Nicky, their leaders. They sat down in the front three rows and looked about them: they had come looking for a fight.

David pushed Mary on to the stage, hoping that a song would calm things down, but it didn't. David walked to the centre of the stage, his heart racing. Then he had a brainwave. 'We're going to do something different tonight,' he said. 'We're going to ask the Mau Mau to take up the collection.' David looked straight at Nicky, one of their leaders, and asked for volunteers. Nicky signalled to five gang members to help, and together they marched to the front. David handed them the collection 'plates' and told them to bring them around behind a curtain and up on to the stage when they had finished the collection. Behind the curtain there was a door to the street.

While the organ played, Nicky and his boys took up the collection. With sixteen stabbings to his name, Nicky did well as a fund-raiser. He signalled to the other gang members and they went behind the curtain. Everyone waited. No one expected to see the money again. Then the room froze as Nicky and the others appeared. 'Here's your money, preacher,' Nicky said.

Then David spoke about the love of God, but his message did not seem to get through, so he prayed. In the silence he heard someone crying. David opened his eyes and saw Israel tugging at a handkerchief and Nicky trying to hold back the tears.

'If you want to have your life changed, now is the time. Stand up and come forward!' said David.

Israel didn't hesitate. He stood up and faced his gang. 'When I say go, you go! Right?'

'Right!' said the Mau Maus. 'Well, I'm going now and you're coming along. Get on your feet!' They followed Israel forward. In fact, they raced him, elbowing each other to get there first. David looked to see if Nicky was among them. He was.

The Ramnad News

Shock housing development

A new church for the Christians of Puliyur was opened today by the local Konar headman, who has reportedly given financial support to the project. The church is the centre of 27 small houses built with the help of a Christian initiative. In a surprising move, 15 of the houses are for Hindu families, while only 12 of the houses are for Christians who come from the Dalit group (untouchables). Each tenant will also be given one acre of land to cultivate.

The seeds of this project were sown several years ago in the 1950s when a 10-year-old Dalit boy was allegedly beaten to death by Konar youths because he said he was too tired to work for them. Trouble between these two groups is common. Tensions were at an all-time high recently when a group of Konars accused a group of Dalits of stealing their cattle. They demanded the Dalits pay a fine or surrender their homes, but although some paid up, other Dalit groups, like the Paraiyars (also untouchables), refused. Instead, they sent word to the Christians in a nearby village that they wanted to join them and become Christians too.

In response, a leader from the Christian community was sent to share the Christian message with the Paraiyars and prepare them for baptism, but the harassment continued, with the leader himself receiving threats on his life.

Things came to a head when two hundred Konars raided the Dalit houses, attacking people with knives and beating them up. Despite their injuries, the Paraiyars have refused to give up their new faith. Since these incidents Paraiyar children have been receiving schooling through their Christian contacts and they have developed a new sense of dignity and worth. This has even won some of them the respect of their Konar neighbours.

The Paraiyars have been accused of converting to Christianity just for what they can get out of it, but as one elderly Christian from Puliyur put it: 'We trust in Jesus, and so God has been with us. We have discovered something precious that we are not about to give up.' The argument seems set to continue, but the presence of the Konar chief at the church opening is an encouraging sign.

From our Chief Correspondent for Religious Affairs: Ramnad District

STIMULUS SHEET 4.5
'Every face tells a story'

Read through the comments below, which might have been made by different people who were caught up in events at Puliyur. Then choose one comment you **agree** with and one you **disagree** with. Complete the unfinished sentences in the box at the foot of the page and then compare your answers with one other person.

> 'We aren't going to pay the Konars for cattle we didn't steal.'
>
> *A Paraiyar*

> 'We are not afraid of the Konars because we have the protection not just of other men, but of God.'
>
> *A Dalit Christian*

> 'You Dalits converted to Christianity just for what you can get.'
>
> *A Konar*

> 'We trust Jesus and so God has been with us.'
>
> *A Dalit Christian*

> 'We don't want Christian leaders coming here. You shouldn't interfere in our business.'
>
> *A Konar youth*

1. I **agree** with the .... who said that...
.... because ....
....
....

2. I **disagree** with the .... who said that ....
.... because ....
....
....

Option 3: **Facing persecution**

SUMMARY

This material tackles the issue of persecution. Why do people sometimes oppose missionary work? It focuses on the story of the murder of missionary medical worker Graham Staines and his two sons. Understanding the issues lying behind this tragedy will help students to grapple with the depth of resentment that conversion can cause. Students will also be challenged to consider their own attitude towards change, especially when it means facing the possibility of opposition or hardship.

LEARNING OUTCOMES

It is expected that, through using this material, students will:

- reflect on what causes people to change their faith;

- be able to explain why changing religion can cause controversy and bring persecution.

RESOURCES REQUIRED

- Stimulus Sheet 4.6: The Graham Staines story (1 between two, main activity, student tasks)

- Stimulus Sheet 4.7: A ranking diamond (1 each, student tasks)

EXTRA RESOURCES AVAILABLE ON CD-ROM

- Photographs of the Staines family

TEACHING STEPS

INTRODUCTORY DISCUSSION

1. Ask students if they can recall any Members of Parliament changing party. Brainstorm the reasons why MPs are driven to take such drastic action: this could include things like disagreement over key issues, the government not keeping its election pledges, or a change in policy. Talk about the kind of dilemma an MP would face when trying to make their mind up what to do and the pressures of making such a decision. Are there other examples where 'changing sides' would create hostility?

2. A closer parallel to the situation in India might be drawn with the situation in Northern Ireland, where to change sides, from Protestant to Catholic or vice versa, is almost inconceivable to most people and could be potentially life-threatening. Just as in Northern Ireland one is born and remains a Protestant or a Catholic, so in India most people are born Hindus, and cannot conceive of ever being anything else.

3. Ask students to think about their own attitudes to others changing their allegiance (to a group, a football club, etc.). How do they react to this type of change? (They do not have to share this.) What about 'grassing' on someone who one knows is doing wrong? Mention could be made of 'whistle blowing' in the world of business.

MAIN ACTIVITY

1. Explain that in some parts of the world people face persecution for changing their faith. People who share their faith with others may also face persecution. (Point out that most, if not all, religious groups have their extremists, but most ordinary believers do not condone the use of violence, preferring to make a peaceful protest.)

2. This section raises the issue of rights to freedom of speech and freedom of religion. Ask students to draw up a charter of rights that focuses on how a country or community should protect people's rights.

   Selected paragraphs from the Universal Declaration of Human Rights might provide a useful framework for this activity; reference could be made especially to Articles 1, 2, 3, 5, 6, 7, 12, 23, 26(B). Discuss the appropriateness and relevance of these articles in this situation. The Declaration can be found on the website of Amnesty International:
   www.amnestyusa.org/udhr

3. Using Stimulus Sheet 4.6, familiarize students with the Graham Staines story. (Colour photographs can be seen on the CD-ROM.) This will need sensitive handling. Point out that it was Indians who tried to save the family, at great risk to themselves. The Staines had lived in India for years and had many friends in the Indian community. Their murder was the act of extremists.

4. One Indian likened the deaths of the Staines to the assassination of Mahatma Gandhi. An Indian newspaper, *The Hindu*, called for protection of Christians when a similar incident happened to a group of Christian Dalits. Why do you think ordinary Indians reacted in this way?

5. Allocate student tasks.

STUDENT TASKS

Level 3–4 Task

(standard achievement age 11)

Ask students to imagine that a book is being written about the martyrdom of Graham Staines and his two sons. It is to be a tribute to his life and to the people of India whom he served. They should design a suitable jacket for the book and write the text for the back cover in order to convey not only the information the book contains but also the issues it raises. They will also need to decide on a suitable title that reflects the Staines' feelings about the people of India and what happened.

Level 5–6 Task

(standard achievement age 14)

Ask students to draw an outline of a head. Inside the outline, they should list the tensions in the minds of those who were involved in the Staines incident. They should write single words or short phrases to represent what was going on in the minds of these people. In what ways is a person's thinking and feeling likely to conflict over this issue?

The students should then write a suitable epitaph for Graham Staines and/or his sons. It should reflect the desire of the family for reconciliation and understanding between people of different faiths.

Level 7–8 Task

(standard achievement age 16)

Explain that some people react badly to members of their community changing their faith because of the way they interpret this 'leaving'. Ask students to use the ranking diamond on Stimulus Sheet 4.7 to rank statements in order of importance in causing this reaction. They should give reasons for their judgement. Ask them then to compare their diamond with another person's and discuss the differences.

Gifted and Talented

Explain that some Hindu Indians react badly to Christians because they think you have to be Hindu to be properly Indian. Do students think that a culture and a faith go together, or can they be separate things? Ask them to think through these issues in relation to the following statistics about India:

India has a population of about 1.1 billion people. Of these:

   80% are Hindu
   14% are Muslim
   2.4% are Christian
   2% are Sikh
   0.7% are Buddhists
   0.5% are Jain
   0.4% belong to other religions

Ask students what they think of the statement: 'India is a Hindu country'. What might it mean for a Christian to be described as 'Indian'? Are there any parallels between the Indian situation and other situations in the news?

Reflection (all levels)

Ask students to consider what they would say if someone asked them to describe themselves in terms of their identity. What would come first? What would be lower down on the list? Would religion form any part of their identity? Can they imagine any circumstances where they would be willing to change their identity to the degree that they faced opposition?

The Graham Staines story

One of the worst attacks on Christians in 1999 took place on 23rd January in the village of Manoharpur in Orissa, India, when an Australian missionary and his two young sons were murdered. Here is their story:

Missionary worker Graham Staines (57) from Australia was travelling with his sons Philip (10) and Timothy (8). He decided to take a stop in the village of Manoharpur and they soon fell asleep in their jeep. As they slept, a mob of about 50 people, armed with axes and other weapons, gathered around the jeep. They had heard about Graham's work and how he shared his Christian faith. The crowd grew angry and people started shouting. Someone threw petrol over the jeep and Graham and the two boys were trapped inside. The villagers tried to stop the attackers, but the mob turned on them and drove them away. Graham and his two young sons burned to death.

This terrible incident was soon being talked about all over India. Graham was well known. Since first coming to India in 1965, he had worked in a home for 60 leprosy patients in Baripada. Graham's wife, Gladys, worked alongside him there and the family had made it their home.

When news of the murders reached Australia, family and friends begged Gladys to return with her daughter. But she was determined to carry on. 'Graham would not have wanted me to pack up and walk away from the leprosy home. Baripada is *my* home.'

Gladys Staines has said publicly that she has forgiven Dare Singh, the man who led the attack. Her act of forgiveness has made a great impression on many Hindus. A Hindu police commissioner who attended one of the many memorial services held for Graham Staines and his sons commented, 'She is a remarkable one – a great Christian'.

Photographs are available on the CD-ROM.

A Ranking Diamond

Cut up the diamond and look at the statements in each section. The issue you are considering is people's reaction to members of their community changing their faith.
Rearrange the pieces to make the same diamond shape, putting the most important statement at the top, the next two below, and so on.

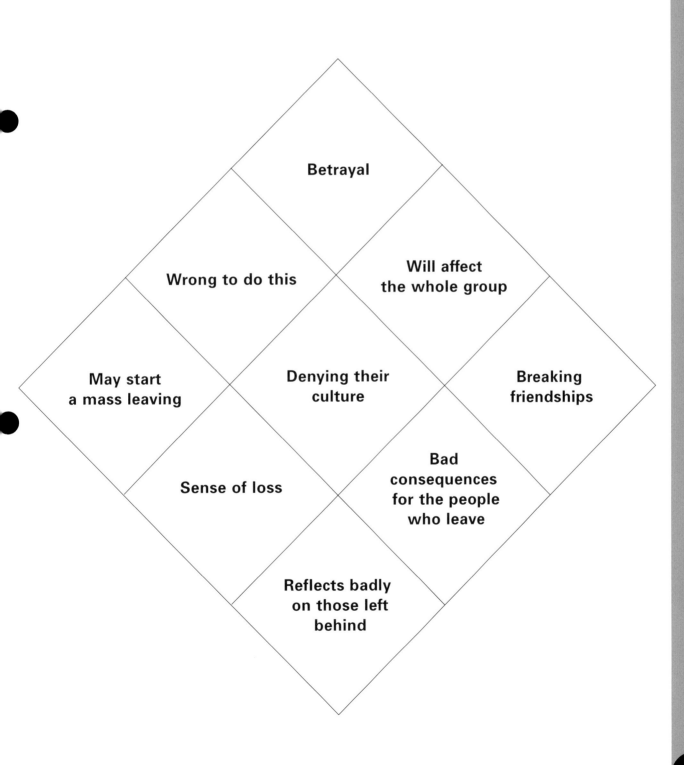

Theme 5: **Keeping body and soul together**

THEME OVERVIEW *In this theme, students reflect on the link between body and soul, the material and the spiritual. They will be asked to consider the Christian commitment to improving the material conditions of other people that is expressed through the Jubilee 2000 campaign. This is a commitment shared with people of other faiths and none. They will also be asked to reflect on a view of life which treats the material and the spiritual as intimately linked through a study of liberation theology, as expressed in the lives of Benedita da Silva and Oscar Romero. Students will also have the option of looking at the Pentecostal movement and liberation theology as two movements that link bodily and spiritual well-being. The purpose of these two studies is to introduce students to different approaches to developing a holistic view of the human being.*

Two controversial questions underpin the material in this theme:

1. *Is it wrong for people to be attracted to Christianity because it fulfils their spiritual or material needs?*

2. *Is there any link between our physical well-being and our spiritual life?*

> The material provided is:
>
> **Option 1:** Meeting other people's needs: dealing with debt
>
> **Option 2:** Sickness and health: physical or spiritual need?
>
> **Option 3:** Liberation

LEARNING OUTCOMES

It is expected that, through using this material, students will:

- understand the concept of a Christian holistic approach to life (Options 1, 2 and 3);

- understand the concept of liberation as expressed by the Christian Church (Option 3);

- learn about the work of Jubilee 2000 (Option 1);

- consider their own views on world debt (Option 1);

- encounter a non-western view of the link between physical and spiritual health (Option 2);

- learn something about Pentecostal Churches (Option 3);

- reflect on the links between the spiritual and the material realms in their own lives (Option 2);

- reflect on the ways in which needs are fulfilled (Option 3).

GLOSSARY

Favela A shanty town in a Brazilian city.

Holistic An integrated view of the person, that views the spiritual, the physical and the psychological as interdependent.

Liberation To be set free from constraints. In liberation theology this reflects a concern to free people from oppressive influences such as poverty, political tyranny and so forth. The Exodus of the Jewish people from Egypt under Moses' leadership is an important inspiration for liberation theology.

Marxism A way of thinking based on the ideas of Karl Marx, that emphasizes class struggle and revolution as the main means of achieving social justice for the oppressed.

Nganga A professional diviner-healer in Africa, often misleadingly called a witchdoctor.

Reincarnation The rebirth of the soul in a new body.

Option 1: **Meeting people's needs: dealing with debt**

SUMMARY

This material looks at some of the problems faced by third-world countries struggling to repay the huge debts that they have accumulated in the form of loans from richer nations. It illustrates the way the burden of debt has left their governments with no alternative other than to divert resources away from health and education into servicing their debts. It highlights the Jubilee 2000 campaign as a western response to this crisis that was widely supported by Christians. This campaign illustrates a Christian holistic view of human beings that embraces the need to change the material circumstances of the poor by attacking a key cause of poverty. This reflects a development in thinking about Christian mission in that:

- it stresses that mission is not a purely spiritual ministry seeking to save people's souls but is concerned with their total human condition;

- it aims to help people address their material needs through the work of aid agencies such as Christian Aid, CAFOD and TEAR Fund;

- it emphasizes the importance of correcting the structural problems that create poverty and not simply helping the human casualties that poverty creates.

This action parallels the work of the earlier missionary movement in its opposition to slavery. Missionaries witnessed the evils of the trade at first hand. The information they sent back was one of the factors that stimulated the campaign to abolish the slave trade.

LEARNING OUTCOMES

It is expected that, through using this material, students will:

- understand the concept of a Christian holistic approach to life;

- learn about the work of Jubilee 2000;

- consider their own views on world debt.

RESOURCES REQUIRED

- Stimulus Sheet 5.1: International Debt (1 between two, main activity)

- Stimulus Sheet 5.2: Jubilee 2000 (1 between two, student tasks)

EXTRA RESOURCES AVAILABLE ON CD-ROM

- Websites with information on third-world debt

- Websites for aid agencies

- Debt and AIDS

- AIDS in Africa

TEACHING STEPS

INTRODUCTORY DISCUSSION

1. Remind the class that early missionary work (in the late eighteenth and the nineteenth centuries) put great emphasis on sharing the message of Jesus Christ through Bible teaching. However, it also became involved in defending the interests of oppressed groups such as slaves in the West Indies. The abolition of slavery in the British Empire would not have happened without the work of Christian missions. Today, perhaps the worst form of oppression is the slavery of international debt, which holds millions of people in a bondage that is just as real as was plantation slavery in the early nineteenth century.

2. Share ideas about the work of Comic Relief or other major fund-raising initiatives. These illustrate the widespread concern that people have to make life better for others. Introduce the familiar notion of aid as providing basic amenities like water, medicines and hospitals, as part of Christian commitment (James 1:27, Matthew 25:40). Mention the work of organizations like TEAR Fund, CAFOD and Christian Aid as examples of a Christian holistic concern for people. Students could be directed to the appropriate websites on the CD-ROM.

Theme 5: Keeping body and soul together

3. Explain that the activity that follows is designed to illustrate a more recent approach that has attracted support from Christians, amongst others.

MAIN ACTIVITY

1. Explain that over the past few years, third-world debt has become a very big issue, with many people appealing for its cancellation, and that the 'Jubilee 2000 Coalition' was formed to campaign for this aim. This group's supporters believed that because the interest on these debts is so high, countries have effectively paid back what they owed many times already. They successfully argued that the richer countries didn't really need the money so the debt should be written off. Use Stimulus Sheet 5.1 to open up this issue and discuss the problems/possibilities that it raises. Explain terms such as 'declared bankrupt', as necessary.

2. Make sure students understand the connection between the debt issue and the resulting lack of resources to educate and help treat diseases such as AIDS in many poorer countries. Teachers may wish to make an OHT of the 'Debt and AIDS' sheet on the CD-ROM.

3. Give students a copy of Stimulus Sheet 5.2 and allocate student tasks.

4. Explain that Jubilee 2000 has now ceased to exist. Its work is being carried forward by Jubilee + and the Jubilee Debt Campaign (UK). Their website details are on the CD–ROM.

Note Tear Fund has produced an excellent resource called 'President for a Day', which teachers might wish to use to follow up some of the themes raised by this activity. For the address see the CD-ROM.

STUDENT TASKS

Level 3–4 Task

(standard achievement age 11)

Ask students to design a poster that reflects the themes of the Jubilee 2000 campaign. They should include some of the ideas from the Bible about the Jubilee. They will need to decide whom the poster is aimed at, what its focus will be and what effect they want it to have. Ask them to predict questions that people may ask about debt cancellation as a result of their poster.

Level 5–6 Task

(standard achievement age 14)

Ask students to read Elizabeth's story on Stimulus Sheet 5.2 and to look for the following:

- her motives;
- what influenced her to join;
- the strategies used in the protests to get the message across.

Using what they have learned about protest, they should design a campaign of their own that will get the Jubilee message across. Ask them to predict questions that people may ask and suggest some answers.

Level 7–8 Task

(standard achievement age 16)

Ask students to write a poem or drama script that will communicate one aspect of the message of Jubilee 2000. (This activity is differentiated by output rather than content and can therefore be used at several levels.)

A suggestion might be to write a diamante poem, in which line 1 has one word, line 2 two words, line 3 three words, line 4 four words (with a turning point in the content of the poem), line 5 three words, line 6 two words, line 7 one word.

Example:

> Chains,
> iron-tight
> choke hope's breath.
> Death-debt is cancelled.
> New life rises.
> Burdens free
> fall.

As an alternative, ask students to use the information on the stimulus sheets and the websites on the CD-ROM to organize a debate on the subject of debt cancellation.

Gifted and Talented

Ask students to imagine that they have been asked to explain to a church's members why they should support the Jubilee + campaign. They should prepare a presentation that will last five minutes. Remind them that this audience will want to know why they as Christians should be supporting this campaign. Students should draw on both stimulus sheets and material from the websites on the CD-ROM. They should think about the different ways they could present the information. They need to prepare a presentation that will be persuasive but not one that will make people feel guilty or under pressure. They can use any form of technology that is practical for the situation.

Reflection (All levels)

Ask students to look again at Elizabeth's story and consider how they would react if Elizabeth and her friends invited them to join a future event. Are there other issues that would move them to action in the way that Elizabeth was moved to join Jubilee 2000?

STIMULUS SHEET 5.1
International Debt

For these activities, you should work in pairs.

ACTIVITY 1

Read the following:

- Aid is given to the poorer countries by governments of other, richer countries and by voluntary agencies, including Christian organizations such as Christian Aid, CAFOD and Tear Fund, that give money and set up projects to tackle particular needs.

- Many countries owe large amounts of money, which they borrowed from richer countries and now have to repay, both the debt and the interest.

- Some countries now owe so much that they will never be able to repay their debts.

Discuss the following three options and decide which one you would vote for and why:

1. Countries should keep repaying their debt and interest.

2. The interest should be reduced.

3. Their debt should be cancelled completely.

ACTIVITY 2

Now read the information that follows. Then discuss whether your vote would change in the light of it.

- In 2000 the UK gave 0.29% of its gross national product in government aid.

- Half of the money donated by the UK in aid is given back in debt repayment.

- Poor countries were encouraged to borrow.

- Interest rates increased soon after they borrowed.

- Prices that poorer countries were paid for the goods they produced went down.

- The debt grew rather than lessened.

- To pay back the debt many countries had to reduce spending on health and education. This has serious consequences for countries coping with AIDS.

- Some governments misused the money they borrowed – for example, to wage war.

- If an individual gets into serious debt they are declared bankrupt. Countries do not have this option.

Jubilee 2000

- Jubilee 2000 was an international movement in over 40 countries, advocating a debt-free millennium for a billion people. Jubilee 2000 in the UK was a coalition of over 80 organizations. They campaigned for a one-off cancellation of the debts of the world's poorest countries.

- 'Jubilee' is a principle that comes from the Bible. A jubilee was a day of release every fiftieth year. In a jubilee year the following happened:

  It was a year of rest for the land and people.

  Slaves were set free.

  Debts were cancelled. (These were often in the form of people who had been sold into slavery for debt.)

  Land was shared out.

- Many Christians supported the Jubilee 2000 campaign. They thought it reflected the spirit of the biblical jubilee and Jesus' care for the poor (Matthew 25:31–45).

Note Although Jubilee 2000's timed campaign finished at the end of 2000, it has now moved into its next phase. 'Jubilee +' and Jubilee Debt Campaign (UK) have taken over its work.

Elizabeth's story

"I heard about the Jubilee 2000 campaign at school, from a visiting speaker. My friends and I felt it was terrible that rich countries such as Britain should demand debts to be repaid from third world countries when the money was desperately needed to improve health and education. So we decided to get involved. We went around the school collecting signatures for a Jubilee 2000 petition and got a few hundred names. We sent letters and campaign cards to various political leaders and generally made people in the school aware of the issues involved.

A few of us also decided to go along to join in the 'Human Chain' at the G8 Summit in Birmingham, in May 1998. G8 Summits are where the world's eight most powerful leaders meet together to discuss important financial issues. In 1998 protesters gathered outside their meeting place to ask them to cancel the third-world debt. 70,000 people were there in total and we all linked arms in a 'human chain' to encourage the leaders to break the chains of debt.

Everyone was dressed in red ('in the red' being a metaphor for being in debt), some were even painted completely red. People had come from all over the world. In particular, there were many church groups present, who had been praying as well as campaigning for change. As a Christian, I thought it was excellent that it enabled me to put my Christian principles into practice.

I am pleased that I got involved in this whole campaign. When I hear of new developments, I feel proud that I helped to make a difference. The G8 countries have not agreed to cancel all of the debts yet, although most have proposed either reducing the interest rates or cancelling part of the debt. However, the campaign is still going on and everyone is hoping that the right decision will be made eventually."

Option 2: **Sickness and health: physical or spiritual need?**

SUMMARY

In the third world, disease, calamitous events, accidents and premature death are much closer to the everyday experience of people than they are for people in the West. This material explores attitudes and beliefs about sickness, health and healing in the third world. It also examines the idea held by many people in Africa and other parts of the world that there is a clear connection between physical and spiritual health and that the body and spirit cannot be separated into rigid compartments. This holistic approach has led in some cases to the blurring of boundaries between healer-diviners (witch doctors), Christian faith healers and medical doctors. This raises questions about the wisdom of the western approach, which usually separates the healing of the body from the healing of the spirit. It is in churches where a more holistic approach to body and spirit has been encouraged that the greatest growth in attendance has been seen. (This can be linked to theme 1.)

LEARNING OUTCOMES

It is expected that, through using this material, students will:

- understand the concept of a Christian holistic approach to life;

- encounter a non-western view of the link between physical and spiritual health;

- reflect on the links between the spiritual and the material realms in their own lives.

RESOURCES REQUIRED

- Bibles (1 between two, level 3–4 only)

- Stimulus Sheet 5.3: The Glenn Hoddle story (1 between two, introduction)

- Stimulus Sheet 5.4: Sickness, salvation and healing (1 between two, student tasks)

- Stimulus Sheet 5.5: Questions for group discussion (1 per group, main activity; the sheets should be cut up so that each group has a set of cards)

EXTRA RESOURCES AVAILABLE ON CD-ROM

- Sickness, salvation and healing (extra information)

- Photograph – A man seeks help from the diviner in northern Benin

- Photograph – Divination with cowry shells and the two halves of a kola nut at a shrine in northern Benin

- Poster showing a man with 'two heads' looking in two different directions – at the church one way and at the traditional diviner healer the other

TEACHING STEPS

INTRODUCTORY DISCUSSION

1. Use Stimulus Sheet 5.3 to initiate a discussion on whether Glenn Hoddle should have been forced to resign and on the issues this story raises.

2. Glenn Hoddle appeared to say that physical disability was some sort of punishment for sins committed in a previous life. That idea is wholly unacceptable to Christians and many other people. (Jesus denied that somebody born blind was being punished for his sins or his parents' sins, see John 9:1–3a.) But that does not necessarily mean there is no relationship between a person's spiritual and physical health. In what ways could the two be linked? Ask the students for ideas and use these as a focus for discussion.

MAIN ACTIVITY

1. Explain that many people all over the world and from a variety of different faith backgrounds believe in the inter-relatedness of the body and the spirit. Stimulus Sheet 5.4 can be used to acquaint students with the way many Africans see the body and spirit as related. (Teachers may wish to consult the longer version of this sheet on the CD-ROM. Visuals on the CD-ROM can also be used.)

2. Give each group a plastic cup containing a complete set of the cards on Stimulus Sheet 5.5. The first person in the group pulls out a question that they then have to respond to. When they have given their response and the reasons for it, they keep that question until the end and the cup is passed on to the next person, who takes another question and so on until everyone has had a turn.

3. Bring the class back together at the end and share some of their responses to the questions.

4. Allocate student tasks.

STUDENT TASKS

Level 3–4 Task
(standard achievement age 11)

Ask students to read the story of the paralysed man (Mark 2:1–12). Then ask them to consider why Jesus both *healed* the paralysed man and *forgave* him. They should imagine that this story has just been told on the radio and they are manning the phones on a 'phone-in' programme. What calls would they expect in response to this story? How would they answer them?

Level 5–6 Task
(standard achievement age 14)

As for level 3–4, but ask students to imagine that their radio programme is also being heard in Africa.

They should read Stimulus Sheet 5.4. Ask them to write down a question that an African Christian might phone in. They should also describe how the presenter might respond to it.

Level 7–8 Task
(standard achievement age 16)

Ask students, working in groups, to write role-play cards for an African and a European debating attitudes to illness. They should draw on the issues raised in earlier discussions. Stimulus Sheet 5.4 can be used for information. They should use the cards to enact the role-play. Afterwards they should de-brief the players and assess how well their cards worked. Did the players have enough information? (Extra information can be found on the CD-ROM.)

Gifted and Talented

Ask students to read the stimulus sheets, then create a series of diagrams to represent the different ways in which body and spirit (and mind) *could* interact. Could the interaction go both ways? (Extra information can be found on the CD-ROM.)

Reflection (All levels)

Ask students to consider, now they have studied this material, how they feel about the interaction between the body and the spirit. Would they ever feel that prayer was an appropriate response to illness?

STIMULUS SHEET 5.3
The Glenn Hoddle story

Glenn Hoddle is thought by some to have been the best footballer ever to play for Tottenham Hotspur. He knew what success was. He went on to become the England manager, steering the team through the World Cup in 1998. He then became manager of Southampton, returning to Spurs as manager in 2001.

Glenn had a good friend called Eileen Drewery, who was a faith healer. She convinced him that links could be made between the physical and the spiritual. He came to believe that some physical problems, such as those encountered by players in the England squad, could be treated or helped by Eileen and her powers as a faith healer. Sometimes he took her along to training sessions and encouraged the England players to consult her. Some players were treated successfully by Eileen, but others refused to have anything to do with her.

Glenn often talked openly about his belief in reincarnation and spirits. Then one day, in a casual conversation with a journalist, he made a comment that seemed to suggest that disabled people were in some way being punished for things they had done in a previous life. His remark was seen as a slur on the disabled. There was a public outcry. A number of people, including government ministers, called for him to be sacked. A few days later, he was forced to resign from his job as England manager.

ACTIVITY
Read through the comments below. Which do you agree/disagree with? Why?

> I think Hoddle's comments were well out of order – especially for someone in his position. He deserved everything he got.

> I don't think Glenn should have lost his job over this. His views had nothing to do with his ability to do the England manager's job.

> If Glenn and some of the England players wanted to consult a faith healer, I can't see anything wrong in that.

> I think the media blew the whole thing out of proportion.

> Glenn should have kept his mouth shut and his views to himself. He should not have involved his players in this faith healing stuff.

STIMULUS SHEET 5.4
Sickness, salvation and healing

In Africa the traditional approach to healing emphasizes the spiritual as a way of healing the body. Africans see healing as something that involves the body, the mind and the spirit. The traditional response to illness was to call in a spiritual expert of some sort: in most cases this would be the diviner-healer, or the witchdoctor, as they are usually known in the West.

Minor ailments, like toothache or a cold, are not seen as requiring a spiritual explanation, but more serious illnesses, unexpected misfortunes or death have traditionally been put down to spirits or curses.

Some years ago there was a cholera outbreak along the River Congo in what is now the Democratic Republic of Congo.

Democratic Republic of Congo

The missionary doctors knew that the main cause was people drinking polluted water but they found it hard to convince local people, including some Christians. People thought that someone had put a spell on the community. This meant that they were reluctant to take the practical measures that would have ended the epidemic. When Christian missionaries arrived, they challenged this linking together of the spiritual and the physical. They introduced western medicine with its emphasis on finding the physical causes of sickness. As the Christian message spread, so did western forms of medicine. However, the missionary hospitals could not cope with demand and in many areas, traditional beliefs and methods have survived.

In some churches, the traditional African idea of healing the person rather than the sickness has been kept, but adapted. Jesus Christ is seen as the healer who heals the whole person – body, mind and spirit. Such churches give healing a prominent position. They normally accept western medicines where appropriate, but only as part of a wider cure. Jesus offers what in the past the traditional healer was expected to provide.

Questions for group discussion

How would you describe a healthy person? Is there more to it than just being physically fit?

What do you understand by the statement 'healing the whole person'?

What makes people ill?

'It is a good thing that people in the West are now recognizing that there is a link between a person's physical and spiritual health.' Do you agree?

Western treatments and medicines have their limitations as well as their successes. What are they?

Is there a similarity between the traditional African approach to illness – that is, to treat the person rather than the illness – and some of the so-called 'alternative' therapies and treatments now available in the West?

Do you think that God sometimes hears and answers prayers for people to be healed directly by him rather than through the medical services?

What is spiritual healing? Is it the same as physical healing?

In what way would accepting the idea of physical health being related to spiritual health affect your own attitude to fitness?

Option 3: **Liberation**

SUMMARY

The final section in this theme looks at the influential Latin-American Christian concept of liberation. It focuses on the life and work of Benedita da Silva, a Pentecostal Christian leader in Rio de Janeiro. A key question it raises is: Is it right for people to be attracted to Christianity because it fulfils their needs?

LEARNING OUTCOMES

It is expected that, through using this material, students will:

- understand the concept of a Christian holistic approach to life;

- understand the concept of liberation as expressed by the Christian Church;

- learn something about Pentecostal Churches;

- reflect on the ways in which needs are fulfilled.

RESOURCES REQUIRED

- *Either* Stimulus Sheet 5.6: Benedita da Silva *or* Stimulus Sheet 5.7: Oscar Romero (1 between two, main activity/student tasks)

- *Either* Stimulus Sheet 5.8 Liberation Theology *or* Stimulus Sheet 5.9: Pentecostalism (1 between two, student tasks)

- Advertisements for a variety of products from newspapers and magazines (introduction)

EXTRA RESOURCES AVAILABLE ON CD-ROM

- Websites on Benedita da Silva, Oscar Romero, and liberation theology

- Video clip of a Pentecostal service

- Extra information on Pentecostal Churches

TEACHING STEPS

INTRODUCTORY DISCUSSION

1. Before the lesson gather a collection of advertisements for a variety of products from newspapers and magazines. Look for adverts that claim to meet particular needs.

2. Give one advert to each pair of students. Ask them to jot down: (1) the name or type of product or service offered; (2) what it is claimed it will do for you. Ask them to discuss briefly who might buy that product and why. Would they themselves buy it? Why/why not? What should emerge from the discussion is the idea that their reaction may depend on whether or not they need what the advert is offering.

3. Talk about the fact that in western society we are used to being able to use our money to fulfil our needs. The crisis comes when people realize that they cannot buy something that is very important to them – for instance, the health of their child. This is part of their everyday experience for people in poorer countries.

4. Explain that in some third-world countries, where people may see little or no hope for the future, many are turning to Christianity to meet their needs. This is particularly the case with churches that are offering a message that combines spiritual hope and physical healing. It is churches like this that are seeing real growth in many countries throughout the world.
(See Theme 1.)

MAIN ACTIVITY

1. Give students either Stimulus Sheet 5.6 or Sheet 5.7 and either Sheet 5.8 or Sheet 5.9.

2. Group students in pairs and ask them to identify key points in either Benedita's life or Oscar Romero's life. Ask them to consider the motivation in this person's life and how their faith affected their work and political life.

3. Allocate student tasks.

STUDENT TASKS

Level 3–4 Task

(standard achievement age 11)

Ask students to imagine that either Benedita or Oscar Romero was to make a speech to the United Nations about her/his life. They should think about what they would have included about their faith, their work for justice and liberation from poverty and oppression.

Ask students to write about the popularity of either Pentecostalism or liberation theology in South America, using either Stimulus Sheet 5.8 or Sheet 5.9.

Level 5–6 Task

(standard achievement age 14)

Ask students to look at either the achievements of Benedita da Silva or the work of Oscar Romero and at the following references: Micah 6:8, Matthew 25:31–40, James 1:27. How do these Bible verses relate to her/his work and in what way can it be described as liberation?

Then ask students to look at either Stimulus Sheet 5.8 or Sheet 5.9 and to write about what needs these movements are fulfilling.

Level 7–8 Task

(standard achievement age 16)

'Liberation is about justice rather than charity'. Ask students to consider how this statement is reflected in Benedita's life. Ask them to do a web search on Benedita and Oscar Romero and select other material that demonstrates the theme of liberation in her/his life. Students should then consider in what ways both liberation theology and Pentecostalism can be seen as forms of liberation. They should draw on the information in Stimulus Sheets 5.8 and 5.9.

Gifted and Talented

Ask students to read Stimulus Sheets 5.8 and 5.9 and to create a summary of the different types of liberation. Explain that it can take many forms. Ask them to consider what western people need liberating from. They will need to think through the different types of oppression that can be experienced. Does this include materialism? Ask students to write a four-minute speech on liberation in modern Britain. Some of the speeches could then be read out.

Reflection (All levels)

Ask students to consider whether western people see themselves as having needs that religion might answer. Do they think that the answer might vary according to age or situation?

STIMULUS SHEET 5.6
Benedita da Silva

Benedita da Silva is a leading politician in Brazil. For years she has been working for the rights of the poor and the oppressed. Her feeling for the poor comes from her own experience:

'I grew up in a favela (shanty town) in Rio. My grandmother had been a slave and my own mother did washing for the rich people. As a young girl, I struggled to deliver the heavy baskets of freshly washed and ironed clothes to the back door of their homes, and being black, I also had to frequently endure the sting of racial insults. By the time I reached my twenties, I had all but given up hope.'

Benedita became a Christian and now belongs to a Pentecostal church. Her faith is her motive for trying to improve people's lives. She had experienced the cruelty endured by many of Brazil's poor people and she felt that God wanted her to do something about it. She did not just want to lessen people's misery; she wanted to change the situation that caused the misery. Benedita became first a nurse's aide then a community volunteer. She also became active in the newly formed Workers Party. She was elected to the Chamber of Deputies in 1990 and in 1994 she became the first black woman to be elected to the Federal Senate.

As a senator Benedita was able to bring about change. She worked on a number of issues that were incorporated into the constitution of Brazil. These included:

- **racial intolerance being regarded as a crime;**
- **120-day pregnancy leave for mothers;**
- **the right of women prisoners to keep their babies while they are breast feeding;**
- **assistance with child care for women with very young children.**

She worked for the government and international organizations on issues such as:

- **children's rights**
- **discrimination against women**
- **teenage and child extermination**
- **mass sterilization of women in Brazil**
- **child prostitution**

Despite this success she continued to live with her family in a simple painted wooden house on a steep hillside on the edge of a *favela*. Living there, she could not fail to be concerned about the issues that affected ordinary people.

Oscar Romero was born in a small town in El Salvador, Central America. From an early age, the poverty of the people around him made him aware that life for most people in El Salvador was a struggle. A few rich people ruled the country and they were kept in power by the military. People who opposed them were often killed by the much feared 'death squads'.

Oscar became a priest and went to work in a poor area. He was very popular, giving food to the hungry and shelter to those without homes. He was promoted and won respect for his work with alcoholics, prisoners and the poor.

As the West got richer, the gap widened between rich and poor countries. The Church felt that this was wrong, because many of the poorer countries were kept in poverty by unfair trading agreements. The Church decided to speak out. In 1968 the Roman Catholic bishops met in Medellín, Colombia. The bishops decided that the Church could not ignore the situation of the people. Injustice was not God's will. The people needed to be liberated from oppression and poverty. Not everyone was happy with this. Some questioned whether the Church should get involved in politics.

Meanwhile, Oscar Romero was promoted again, first to the post of bishop, then to archbishop. Opponents of the government were dismayed. Romero was a gentle, quiet man, and a bookworm. They thought he would never oppose the government.

In 1977 a priest who was a friend of Romero was shot after speaking out against the government. Those in power probably hoped that this murder would frighten Romero into silence: they were wrong. Romero called for an investigation. The government ignored him, so Romero temporarily closed all the schools. He also refused to take part in government ceremonies until the conditions of the people changed. He wrote to the Pope, listing the evils of the government. He wrote to the president of the United States and asked him to stop sending money to the government of El Salvador for they simply used it to oppress the people. He invited soldiers to mutiny and to disobey evil orders.

On 24th March 1980, while he was celebrating Mass, Oscar Romero was shot. The assassins were never caught. The quiet, gentle bookworm had become dangerous. He had moved on from helping the poor to trying to change the situation that caused such poverty and oppression.

El Salvador

STIMULUS SHEET 5.8
Liberation theology

Jesus said that he had come to preach good news to the poor and to release the oppressed. Nowhere is this more relevant than in Latin America, where liberation theology was born. Liberation theology is about:

- **action on behalf of the poor and the oppressed;**

- **political and economic action to help the poor;**

- **changing the structures that create poverty;**

- **seeing the Christian faith as not just a private matter for individuals;**

- **concern with how society is organized;**

- **the inspiration of Marxist thinking.**

During the 1960s a great change took place in the political thinking of many Roman Catholics in South America. They wanted to change the situation of the poor, for they believed that God cared about the whole person: their health, education and way of life, not just the state of their soul. In 1968 many of these ideas were accepted at the conference of the Latin American Bishops of the Roman Catholic Church at Medellín in Colombia.

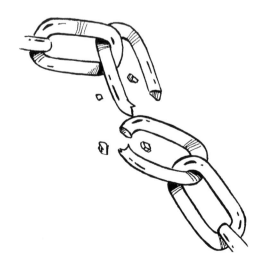

Liberation theology is about action on behalf of the poor. It is about demanding justice, not asking for charity. Many Catholic nuns and priests moved into poor communities and shared their sufferings. This gave them the understanding they needed. They then mobilized communities to change their lives, even if this meant confronting the government.

In Brazil, Argentina and Chile and in many other countries, Christians suffered at the hands of oppressive governments who did not want to change. There were revolutions across South America, but few brought about the justice that people wanted.

Liberation theology did not disappear when some of the revolutions failed; it still had much to teach people. The new liberationists learned from the past. Now they look for a caring response to suffering from any government. They look for a system that will put people first and profit second. They go with whatever brings life and justice. Once they tried to change the whole structure at once, now they often start on a small and local scale.

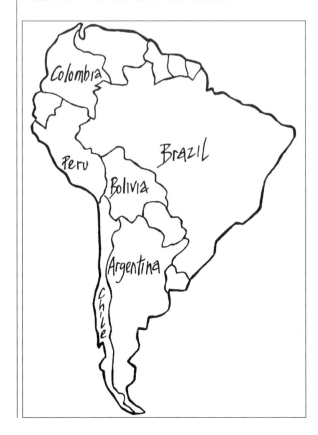

STIMULUS SHEET 5.9
Pentecostalism

Pentecostalism is one of the youngest Christian denominations, but it is growing fast. Over 500 million Christians throughout the world today belong to churches that may broadly be described as Pentecostal. Some analysts predict that Pentecostal Christians may account for 44 per cent of all Christians by the year 2025.

This remarkable growth is based mainly in the third world. The Pentecostal Churches have grown rapidly in Latin America. They have a special appeal to the poor, and are increasingly seen by many scholars as the most relevant religion or 'theology of liberation' for the poor and the oppressed.

What makes Pentecostal Churches particularly popular with the poor?

Worship
They offer worship that takes people away from their everyday situation. The music is lively and the worship is spontaneous – with plenty of participation by the congregation.

Origins
Pentecostalism was born among the African slave communities of the United States and the Caribbean. Many later Pentecostal churches were formed by immigrant communities and lacked the racism that some people experienced in more traditional churches.

Spiritual gifts
Pentecostal Churches give an important place to the exercise of the spiritual gifts and the power of the Holy Spirit. To a community that has little political power, this is important.

Whole people
Many people from the non-western world are attracted to Pentecostal Churches because all of them, in different ways, regard healing as an integral part of their spiritual ministry. They do not see illness as something that happens only to the body; mind and spirit are also involved. This is important to those who have little access to health care.

All of life
Pentecostal Christians emphasize the power of Christ to meet people's everyday needs. Being part of a large faith that stresses the power of God is important to people who feel powerless.

Theme 6: **Women, men and God**

THEME OVERVIEW *In this theme, students encounter the controversial issue of the way in which religious beliefs interact with different cultures, moral frameworks and family structures. The particular focus of this theme is on the role of women in a non-western culture such as Africa, and on how the coming of Christianity changed this. The particular appeal of Christianity to women in traditional African societies is that it liberates them from oppressive relationships with men.*

At first sight the material might seem remote from the experience of most British young people. In fact it raises highly relevant issues, such as, 'Does the value of a woman depend on her ability to be a good wife and mother?' and 'Does western society practise a form of serial polygamy, in which people exchange one marriage partner for another through divorce?'. The study of this material will challenge students to reflect on their own attitudes to the place of women in society. It will also raise the question of how one makes a moral decision in situations where there are no 'perfect' answers – an issue faced by people of all faiths and none. Finally students are asked to reflect on ways in which Christianity might challenge aspects of western culture.

The material provided is:

Option 1: The value of a woman

Option 2: Evaluating polygamy

Option 3: Making difficult choices

LEARNING OUTCOMES

It is expected that, through using this material, students will:

- learn about gender relationships and family structures, especially in relation to the role of women in a non-western culture (Options 1, 2 and 3);

- understand that Christian belief makes a difference to the stance taken on these issues (Options 1, 2 and 3);

- have a better understanding of the effects of polygamy on those involved, especially women (Options 2 and 3);

- know about and be able to comment on some of the problems polygamy presents to society in general and to the Christian Church in particular (Options 2 and 3);

- reflect on their own attitudes towards the role of women in society (Option 1);

- reflect on how values are expressed through behaviour (Option 1);

- consider how difficult moral decisions are made and the relevance to their own moral decision-making (Options 2 and 3).

GLOSSARY

Baptism Initiation ceremony into the Church, involving immersion or sprinkling with water.

Bridewealth The 'price' paid by the prospective husband to the bride's family for the 'purchase' of a bride. The price could be paid in the form of money, cattle or other goods.

Excommunicate To expel someone from church membership or to forbid him or her to take an active part in church services.

Monogamy The practice of having only one husband or wife.

Patriarchal A form of social organization in which males hold most of the power.

Polygamy The practice of having more than one husband or wife. **Serial polygamy** is a phrase introduced to describe the practice of marrying and divorcing several partners, one after the other. This is increasingly common in the western world.

Option 1: **The value of a woman**

SUMMARY

Christians believe that all people, both men and women, have inherent value because they are made and loved by God. This value does not depend on the role a person plays. However, the role given to a woman by society, and therefore her implicit 'value' to that society, is a controversial issue that attracts different responses from different communities. The views of traditional societies often conflict with those of more liberal, westernised ones on this matter, as evidenced, for example, by the anxieties that many British Muslims have about the way girls are educated.

This material examines the Christian belief that men and women are created in the image of God, with the potential to be creative themselves but that a special place is given to motherhood. The value placed on marriage is explored by comparing the cost of a wedding with the practice of 'bridewealth'. Some of the strengths and weaknesses of societies where women tend to be regarded primarily as mothers are also looked at. Students are asked to consider for themselves how they feel about the need to strike the right balance between giving motherhood its proper value and preserving career opportunities for women.

LEARNING OUTCOMES

It is expected that, through using this material, students will:

- learn about gender relationships and family structures, especially in relation to the role of women in a non-western culture;

- understand that Christian belief makes a difference to the stance taken on these issues;

- reflect on their own attitudes towards the role of women in society;

- reflect on how values are expressed through behaviour.

RESOURCES REQUIRED

- Stimulus Sheet 6.1: Women's work? (1 between two, introduction)

- Stimulus Sheet 6.2: Wedding bills? (OHT/1 between two, main activity/student tasks)

- Stimulus Sheet 6.3: Bridewealth and motherhood (1 between two, main activity/student tasks)

EXTRA RESOURCES AVAILABLE ON CD-ROM

- Video clip showing a dowry (bridewealth) of two cows being presented

TEACHING STEPS

INTRODUCTORY DISCUSSION

1. Using Stimulus Sheet 6.1, the girls and boys could separately address the question at the top. Is there any agreement between the two groups?

2. Explain that the passages from Proverbs are particularly relevant for Christians and Jews who draw on the biblical tradition. They see this as combining a high view of motherhood (vv.27–28) with an affirmation of a woman's right to engage in creative work on her own account (vv.13–24). Ask students to complete the questions at the bottom of Sheet 6.1.

3. Discuss the importance of the two different images of a woman as a caring wife and mother and as a woman of enterprise. Make the point that Christianity takes very seriously both aspects of life. It does this through its emphasis on the status of every woman (and every man) as a person created in the image of God, with unique gifts and the potential to be creative themselves both in work and in family life.

4. Introduce the idea that some people and societies place greater emphasis on the role of the woman as wife and mother, while others prefer to promote the image of the successful and enterprising career woman. Can we learn from both examples?

MAIN ACTIVITY

1. Ask students to imagine that a relative or friend is planning their wedding day. The person wants a big traditional western wedding and has asked them to help.

2. If possible, show some up-to-date pictures, advertisements or articles from a recent wedding magazine. Ask students what things a couple planning a big wedding in this country would need to think about in preparation for the big day. How much do they think it will cost? (Estimates for 2000 suggest that it can cost, on average, anything between £4,000 and £10,000.) Use Stimulus Sheet 6.2 and share the findings.

3. Give out Stimulus Sheet 6.3 and discuss the questions.

4. Allocate student tasks.

STUDENT TASKS

Level 3–4 Task
(standard achievement age 11)

Ask students to use the information on Stimulus Sheet 6.3 to make a short list of the good and bad points of African and western approaches to weddings and marriage. They should use their lists to compare the two approaches. How would they justify their conclusions in each case? They could also use the extra material on the CD-ROM.

Level 5–6 Task
(standard achievement age 14)

As for level 3–4, but in addition ask students to design a marriage celebration where the emphasis is put on the value of the woman as a person rather than on the wealth she brings or the material things associated with a wedding. See the extra material on the CD-ROM.

Level 7–8 Task
(standard achievement age 16)

Ask students to write arguments for and against abolishing both bridewealth and very expensive western weddings. The focus should be on teasing out the values these practices express concerning women. The arguments can then be used in a debate. Ask students to suggest alternatives that would reflect:

- a woman's inherent value, regardless of role;
- her value as a creative person;
- her value as a wife and mother.

Gifted and Talented

'Looking at the role of women inevitably reflects on the role of men.' Ask students whether they think this statement is true. They should give reasons for their opinions.

Now ask students to read Proverbs 31:10–31, which is a passage about a 'wife of noble character'. Ask them to conduct a survey to find out people's views on what makes a good husband. A list of the results could then be drawn up and presented in different ways. Students could rewrite the passage in Proverbs, focusing instead on 'a *husband* of noble character'.

Reflection (All levels)

People show their values (not just concerning women) by their behaviour and how they relate to others. Ask students to think about the ways in which they show their values. How can people tell what is important to them?

Show students a wedding ring (or a picture of one). Explain that for some the wedding ring is a symbol of restriction. For others it is a symbol of the unique value placed on a particular relationship. The circular nature of the ring symbolizes a long-term commitment. Ask students to look at the ring. How do they see it?

STIMULUS SHEET 6.1
Women's work?

Look at the two pictures below and ask yourself what view of the worth of a woman is being expressed in each one.

Compare this with what the writer of the Book of Proverbs has to say about a woman he admires.

> She selects wool and flax and works with eager hands. She is like the merchant ships, bringing food from afar. She gets up while it is still dark; she provides food for her family and portions for her servant girls. She considers a field and buys it; out of her earnings she plants a vineyard. She sets about her work vigorously; her arms are strong for her tasks. She sees trading as profitable and her lamp does not go out at night. In her hand she holds the distaff and grasps the spindle with her fingers. She opens her arms to the poor and extends her hands to the needy. When it snows, she has no fear for her household; for all of them are clothed in scarlet. She makes a covering for her bed; she is clothed in linen and purple. Her husband is respected at the city gate, where he takes his seat among the elders of the land. She makes linen garments and sells them, and supplies the merchants with sashes.
>
> Proverbs 31:13–24 (NIV)

> She watches over the affairs of her household and does not eat the bread of idleness. Her children arise and call her blessed; her husband also praises her.
>
> Proverbs 31:27–28 (NIV)

Look at the two extracts above.

1. What do you think the writer is saying about:

    (a) the role of a woman as a wife and mother?

    (b) the right of a woman to engage in creative work on her own account?

2. What do you think about both these things?

Wedding bills?

An expensive wedding is often seen as the ideal start to a marriage. Write down what you think are the approximate costs of the following items. What do you think the total bill might be if a couple decided to have all these things?

- **Dress for bride**

- **Hire of suit for bridegroom**

- **Payment to vicar/church/registrar**

- **Clothes for bridesmaids/pageboys**

- **Hire of hotel for reception**

- **Food and drink**

- **Cars to and from church and reception**

- **Flowers**

- **Honeymoon**

- **Wedding cake**

- **Rings**

- **Video**

- **Photographs**

ACTIVITY *Look at the reasons given below for people choosing this type of wedding. Number the reasons in the order of importance you think they have for people today.*

☐ For the enjoyment of the day and to create a good memory

☐ To make a commitment before God

☐ To make a public show

☐ For the sake of the family

☐ To make a public statement of their commitment

☐ So that people will see how much they value marriage

☐ To show off how much money they have

☐ To get lots of presents in order to start married life

☐ To show others how much they love each other

Think about it

What do you think is the importance of the wedding ceremony in a marriage relationship?

Theme 6: Women, men and God

Bridewealth and motherhood

Bridewealth

Bridewealth is a practice in some African cultures. This is where the husband 'buys' a wife by negotiating a 'price' with the woman's family in the form of money, cattle or other goods. In some parts of Africa, the emphasis is not so much on the relationship between the husband and wife as on the importance of their having children. Indeed, sometimes the wife may be regarded almost as a 'child-bearing machine' that has to be purchased. One Nigerian man, who paid a large bride-price for a wife who later ran away, said he was not too worried because she had left him with four children!

Motherhood

In many African cultures, women find respect as mothers. Motherhood can bring power, reward and prestige, especially when their children do well. But even if the children don't do particularly well, some would say that a woman is only truly fulfilled when she becomes a mother. African children are brought up to hold their mothers in very high regard. Asked who they trusted most, Nigerian students placed mother first, father second and wife third. This illustrates, perhaps, the importance placed on motherhood. It is the means by which men reproduce themselves and continue the family name.

Western parallels

Expensive weddings with all the trimmings are still very popular in the West. In some cases it is as though the cost of the wedding is a measure of the value of the couple's relationship. Is this similar to the practice of bridewealth? Large families are not very common in western societies; the attitude towards children is very different. Here the view is more likely to be that children cost lots of money so it is best not to have too many of them. Motherhood *alone* may be seen as an interference with the ability to earn money. The idea of being content to be 'just a mother' is sometimes looked down upon.

THINGS TO THINK ABOUT

1. Is the practice of bridewealth likely to be responsible for moral and social problems, such as the giving of girls to the highest bidder? Does the high cost of a wedding in Britain also create problems, such as delaying marriage until the wedding can be afforded?

2. Is bridewealth an indication that a man places great value on his wife or is it saying that she is only a means to an end? What about an expensive engagement ring? What does that indicate?

3. What are the strengths and weaknesses of the attitudes to motherhood in African and western societies?

Theme 6: Women, men and God

Option 2: **Evaluating polygamy**

SUMMARY

This material takes polygamy as a case study of a practice which Christians believe is wrong but which is embedded in the way of life of a non-western culture. Polygamy is likely to be culturally alien to the majority of British students, although they may be aware of court cases involving Mormons in America. The material therefore encourages students to reflect on polygamy in the light of the western practice of discarding one marriage partner in favour of another, perhaps younger, partner. The term 'serial' polygamy is introduced as a provocative idea that helps to raise questions about attitudes increasingly taken for granted in the western world.

LEARNING OUTCOMES

It is expected that, through using this material, students will:

- learn about gender relationships and family structures, especially in relation to the role of women in a non-western culture;

- understand that Christian belief makes a difference to the stance taken on these issues;

- have a better understanding of the effects of polygamy on those involved, especially women;

- know about and be able to comment on some of the problems polygamy presents to society in general and to the Christian Church in particular;

- consider how difficult moral decisions are made and the relevance to their own moral decision making.

RESOURCES REQUIRED

- Stimulus Sheet 6.4: Madam and the other woman (1 between two, main activity/student tasks)

- Stimulus Sheet 6.5: Polygamy (1 between two, student tasks)

TEACHING STEPS

INTRODUCTORY DISCUSSION

1. Read out the explanation below of polygamy. Brainstorm students' reactions to it.

   Polygamy, the practice of taking more than one marriage partner, is common in certain parts of the world, especially in agricultural societies where a large family is needed to work the land and where there is little or no welfare provision. In old age, people look to their children to supply their needs and to take care of them. Children are needed to help work the fields, and some will die anyway, so the more the merrier! The need to produce children is probably the most important factor governing marriages in Africa. If the ability to produce children is the major concern of the husband, then polygamy is distinctly advantageous.

2. Now introduce the idea of 'serial polygamy' by reading the quote below. Brainstorm students' reactions to it. Then compare the two reactions.

   Serial polygamy is when one person has more than one marriage partner but has them one after the other. This practice is common in the West. Western people are often critical of polygamy and Africans are often critical of serial polygamy.

MAIN ACTIVITY

1. Divide the class into six groups. Hand out Stimulus Sheet 6.4. Ask three of the groups to prepare a case to support the continuance of polygamy in the African village setting, and the other three groups to prepare a case for abolishing it.

2. Organize a brief debate, letting a spokesperson from each group make one point either for or against the motion: 'Polygamy is not an acceptable way of life in the twenty-first century.' Take a class vote on the issue.

3. Give out Stimulus Sheet 6.5 and allocate student tasks.

(**Note** Students may be aware of polygamy from TV documentaries. There have been some well-publicized programmes on Mormon men with polygamous marriages.)

STUDENT TASKS

Level 3–4 Task

(standard achievement age 11)

Ask students to list ways in which polygamy favours men. In what ways do they think the Church's response also favoured men and failed women? Ask them to consider who serial polygamy favours and why.

Level 5–6 Task

(standard achievement age 14)

The same task as for level 3–4, but ask students also to explore what they think would have been the social and economic results for the discarded 'non-wives' of this insistence on monogamy. Ask students to write a letter from a discarded non-wife explaining what her problems are. They should also consider what problems might be associated with serial polygamy.

Level 7–8 Task

(standard achievement age 16)

Using both stimulus sheets, students should write down what changes they think will be necessary if African society is to move from polygamy to monogamy. For each change, they should give a reason why they think it will be necessary. Ask them to consider whether it is right for westerners to seek to create this change in African culture. Then ask them to consider what changes would be needed in western society to end serial polygamy.

Gifted and Talented

Ask students to look at the criticism of polygamy on the two stimulus sheets. Which of these do they think Africans would draw on to criticize western serial polygamy? How valid do they think these arguments would be?

Reflection (All levels)

Suggest that in the West faithful monogamy is often presented as restricting. Ask students to think of examples of this in films, advertisements and so on. In what ways could marriage to one person be presented as liberating? Ask them to think about their own attitude to faithful monogamy.

STIMULUS SHEET 6.4
Madam and the other woman

*An article called 'Madam and the other woman'
appeared in the* Lagos Sunday Times. *It included points
made by a number of women both for and against the
practice of polygamy.*

FOR

- I now have children and I have resolved not to have any more. My husband is free to marry a second wife if he chooses so that I am free not to have more children.

- I would like my husband to have a second wife instead of a girlfriend outside of marriage.

- I would not object to my husband having a second wife if he were prepared to look after both of us properly.

- I would like someone to help me in my domestic duties that are daily increasing. I would therefore not object to my husband taking another wife.

AGAINST

- I have told my husband that the day he decides to bring in another wife I will move out.

- Our religion says that a man is entitled to four wives. I think there is something wrong with that religion.

- God has designed it that a man should have one wife.

- I do not want my husband to keep a woman outside our matrimonial home or to marry another wife. Since we are Christians we have to stick to the Bible, which teaches that a man should only take one wife.

A trader, Mrs Eunice Nwaosa, said:

"God forbid this bad thing! I cannot stand any of the two (second wife or girlfriend). I married my husband fifteen years ago 'for better, for worse' and I do not think he has ever had any serious complaints against me. I take care of him well and satisfy him in every way. I therefore see no reason why he will want to marry another wife or keep girlfriends outside our marriage."

STIMULUS SHEET 6.5
Polygamy

It has been said that it is usually the man's view on polygamy that is heard. Among the Lugbara people of Uganda, where polygamy is common practice, they have some interesting proverbs that illustrate the attitude of some men towards their wives:

The tongue of co-wives is pointed.

The tongue of co-wives is bitter.

A co-wife is the owner of jealousy!

These proverbs are considered to be 'traditional wisdom'. Many would argue that polygamous families are not the ideal setting in which to bring up children or create a loving environment. The polygamous home can be full of uncertainty and jealousy.

When Christianity came to Africa, it taught that monogamous marriage was the only valid and recognizable form of marriage. Polygamous men who sought baptism were often advised to choose one of the women for a wife and send the others away as 'non-wives'.

Many Christians considered that it was unjust and inhuman for a 'non-wife' to be treated like this. After all, she had been married according to customary law and had lived with her husband probably for several years. Why should she be cast aside simply because the husband desired baptism? Such teaching has resulted in the charge that the Church's concern has been for the polygamous men, but not for the women. Modern feminists oppose polygamy as a system that exploits women for the benefit of men.

Polygamy is still practised throughout Africa, but it is rapidly becoming something that only rich men can afford.

"Freely chosen monogamous marriage – perhaps the supreme irreversible gain which Christianity brought to African women – threatened patriarchal power, both of polygamous husbands and bridewealth-hungry fathers."

Dr Deborah Gaitskell of the Institute of Commonwealth Studies in the University of London

Option 3: **Making difficult choices**

SUMMARY

The practice of polygamy poses enormous challenges for the Christian Church, which teaches that monogamous marriage is the best form of relationship for a man and a woman. This has often made Christianity an attractive religion for African women as it frees them from the abuse of some forms of polygamy. The problem is: what happens when a person involved in a polygamous marriage becomes a Christian? Should they be allowed to participate in communion? Should a polygamous husband who becomes a Christian 'put away' all his wives other than the first wife? This material examines these questions. The case study encourages students to reflect on the general principle that in moral decision-making we should not allow the desire for the very best outcome to get in the way of achieving a compassionate and moral outcome, even if it is not the 'perfect' one.

LEARNING OUTCOMES

It is expected that, through using this material, students will:

- learn about gender relationships and family structures, especially in relation to the role of women in a non-western culture;

- understand that Christian belief makes a difference to the stance taken on these issues;

- have a better understanding of the effects of polygamy on those involved, especially women;

- know about and be able to comment on some of the problems polygamy presents to society in general and to the Christian Church in particular;

- consider how difficult moral decisions are made and the relevance to their own moral decision-making.

RESOURCES REQUIRED

- Stimulus Sheet 6.6: Polygamy and the Church (1 between two, main activity/student tasks)

- Stimulus Sheet 6.7: Men and women on polygamy (1 between two, main activity/student tasks)

TEACHING STEPS

INTRODUCTORY DISCUSSION

1. Talk about situations where every course of action has some drawbacks or is not wholly satisfactory. Students may be able to suggest examples. When faced with this type of decision – where there is no perfect solution – what guides people's actions? As an example, describe what happened during the Second World War when some Christians hid Jews to save them from the Nazis. When asked if there were any Jews in the house, they lied. Lying is wrong for Christians, of course, but in this situation telling the truth would have resulted in the death of others. There was no 'perfect' course of action. This does not make lying right but it was the 'least worst' option or the most compassionate option in the circumstances.

MAIN ACTIVITY

1. Give out Stimulus Sheets 6.6 and 6.7.

2. Discuss what problems arise for the Church concerning polygamy. Do the problems faced by men differ from those faced by women? Focus on one problem to discuss in detail and ask students for suggestions that might lead to its solution.

3. Allocate student tasks.

STUDENT TASKS

Level 3–4 Task
(standard achievement age 11)

Explain that church leaders feel torn by two conflicting ideals:

(a) their desire to be faithful to the Bible's teaching on having one partner in marriage;

(b) their concern for people's well-being, which is also based on the Bible's teaching on love and looking after the family.

Ask students to look up the following references and then to create a diagram that will reflect this internal conflict. They should use the image of a 'tug of war', placing the references on different sides of the rope depending on the direction in which they pull people.

> Genesis 30:1 (Jacob marries two sisters)
>
> 1 Corinthians 13:1–3, 13 (love as supreme)
>
> 1 Corinthians 7:2 (having one wife)
>
> James 1:27 (real religion shown in compassion)
>
> 1 Timothy 5:8 (looking after the family)
>
> 1 Samuel 1:2, 6–7 (trouble among the wives)

Level 5–6 Task
(standard achievement age 14)

As for level 3–4, but instead of the 'tug of war' idea, ask students to create their own image that captures the complexity of this issue. They should write an explanation of their image.

Ask them to look at the conclusion reached by the 1988 Lambeth Conference (on Stimulus Sheet 6.6) and decide whether they agree with this decision. They should give a reason for their answer.

Level 7–8 Task
(standard achievement age 16)

Ask students to look at the conclusion reached by the Lambeth Conference 1988 and to imagine that they have to explain how the Anglican Church reached this conclusion. They should either write a passage or create a diagram with notes to show the factors that led to it. Things they should think about are:

- the experiences of men and women in a polygamous society;
- church-related experiences of Christians in polygamous marriages;
- biblical teaching (see level 3–4 task);
- how people make decisions in difficult situations.

Gifted and Talented

Suggest that the 'least worst' or 'most compassionate' option is one way of making a difficult decision. Ask students to consider what other guidelines they could devise for difficult decision-making. They should use the example of polygamy to illustrate their guidelines.

Reflection (All levels)

Ask students to think of a time when they have had to make a difficult decision and there may have been no 'perfect' option. What guided them? What do they think they could learn from the way the Lambeth Conference handled polygamy in Africa?

Polygamy and the Church

> **"I find it incredible that the Church has been more generous to a divorced person than to a polygamist who intends to continue supporting and caring for his wives and children."**
>
> David Gitari, Anglican Archbishop of Kenya,
> in 'The Church and Polygamy', Transformation 1:1
> (January 1984, p.9)

Most Christians believe that a marriage should be monogamous – that is, one man with one wife. Sometimes Church leaders have insisted that a man should get rid of all but his first wife when he becomes a Christian. In other cases, a polygamous husband or wife may not be allowed to be baptized or to take communion.

David Gitari, the Anglican Archbishop of Kenya, has been quite outspoken on this subject. What do you think he means in the quote above? Do you agree with him?

The 1988 Lambeth Conference upheld monogamy as God's plan for marriage and as the ideal relationship of love between husband and wife. However, it agreed with Archbishop Gitari's proposal that when a polygamous household becomes Christian, the Church should seek to keep the household together. It also said that both men and women should be allowed to be baptized and take communion, although they could not hold any office in the Church.

Paraphrase of the 1988 Lambeth Conference Conclusion

A man who becomes a polygamist before becoming a Christian shall, on becoming a Christian, be baptized with his believing wives and children on condition that he shall not take any other wives. He will not be required to put away any of his wives because to do so would cause them great hardship.

From *The Truth Shall Make You Free: The Lambeth Conference 1988*, Church House Publishing, 1988, pp. 220–221

Men and women on polygamy

WOMEN ON POLYGAMY

I was married to a polygamist when I was young without knowing that it was a sin. I attended baptism classes and I have not yet been baptized, and my children are also not baptized. I love the Lord Jesus who saved me. I would very much like to be baptized and confirmed.

My husband, who is not polygamous, has refused to marry me in church, as this would hinder him from becoming polygamous. The vicar told me that I couldn't be baptized and confirmed unless we have a wedding in church. Since my husband has completely refused a church wedding (he also says it is too expensive), does it mean that I shall never be baptized? Incidentally, I accepted the Lord as my personal Saviour two years ago.

MEN ON POLYGAMY

I was a polygamist before I became a Christian. I was baptized 40 years ago, but I am told I cannot be confirmed until I put away my second wife. I find it difficult to send her away, as she has nowhere to go. She is the mother of my children. I hope the Church will accept me before I die.

I became a Christian when I was young. I was married in church 40 years ago. After living with my wife for ten years, we did not have any children. We both agreed that I should take a second wife so that we could have children. I was then excommunicated. Ten years ago, I accepted the Lord as my Saviour, together with my wives. They take Holy Communion but I was told to wait. I now feel physically weak as I am getting old and I might die any time. Please, Bishop, I do not want to die outside the Church. Please have mercy on me.

Theme 6: Women, men and God

Acknowledgements

The publisher and authors would like to thank the following for permission to reproduce material in this pack.

Introduction

Continuum for 'What is a good thinker' from *Teaching Thinking: Philosophical Enquiry in the Classroom*, by Robert Fisher, p.9 (London, Continuum, 1998)

Theme 1

Three's Company for the map 'Worldwide Growth Rate of Christianity' from *Atlas of the Bible and the History of Christianity* ed. Tim Dowley, pp.138–9

Rev. Taffy Davies for two cartoons from The Tide Is Running Out: What the English Church Attendance Survey Reveals by Dr Peter Brierley (London, Christian Research, 2000)

Lambeth Palace Library for the photograph of Bishops attending the 1867 Lambeth Conference. Library reference: Longley 9,f.2

The Church Times for the photograph of the Bishops attending the 1998 Lambeth Conference, from the cover of EFAC Bulletin, 50 (January 1999)

Theme 2

Masao Takenaka for photograph of Yayu Village Presbyterian Church from *The Place where God Dwells* by Masao Takenaka, p.52 (Auckland, Pace, 1995, in association with Christian Conference of Asia and Asian Christian Art Association)

Meryl Doney for the photograph of an Ethiopian Drummer taken from *Black Angels* by Richard Marsh, p.22 (Lion, 1998)

Asian Christian Art Association for 'Washing the Feet' by Jyoti Sahi from *The Bible Through Asian Eyes* by Masao Takenaka and Ron O'Grady, p.131 (Auckland, Pace, 1991, in association with the Asian Christian Art Association)

Masao Takenaka for 'Jesus Washes Peter's Feet' by Sadao Watanabe, from *Biblical Prints by Sadao Watanabe* by Sadao Watanabe and Masao Takenaka (Shinkyo Shuppanasha, 1986) illus. 39

Hodder & Stoughton for 'African Canticle', 'I have no words to thank you' and 'God free you' from *An African Prayer Book* compiled by Desmond Tutu (London, Hodder & Stoughton, 1995) pp.7, 14; reproduced by permission of Hodder and Stoughton Limited. Includes right to make up to 20 photocopies for classroom purposes.

Masao Takenaka for prayer beginning 'Eternal God, we say good morning to you'

Mothers' Union, London for the prayer of the Church of the Province of Melanesia, beginning 'O Jesus be the canoe'

Sandra Rooney, Mission Education and Interpretation, Wider Church Ministries, United Church of Christ for the Prayer of the Moderator of the Evangelical Presbyterian Church in Ghana, beginning 'Years ago our elders said', and for the Prayer on a Church Wall in Mexico, beginning 'Give us, Señor, a little happiness'. Both are taken from the *Calendar of Prayer* 1986–7 of the United Church of Christ Board for World Ministries, USA.

Bible Reading Fellowship for the Prayer of the Ojibway Nation, beginning 'Grandfather, look at our brokenness' taken from *Our World God's World* edited by Barbara Wood (Oxford, Bible Reading Fellowship,1986)

I-to Loh for 'Wa Wa Wa Emimimo'; text and music transcription and English paraphrase by I-to Loh, used by permission

Gideons International for John 3:16 in various languages. Reproduced by kind permission of the Gideons International in the British Isles, Lutterworth, Leics.

Bible Society for 'Into Many Languages' taken from *Bestseller* © Margaret Cooling, 1997, published by British and Foreign Bible Society

Stainer & Bell Ltd for The Sussex Carol. Material collected and arranged by Ralph Vaughan Williams © 1919 Stainer & Bell Ltd, 23 Gruneisen Road, London, N3 1DZ

Dr He Qi for ANNUNCIATION (Chinese Ink and Colour on Paper). Artist: Dr Prof He Qi, Nanjing Theological Seminary

Christian Herald for the article 'Clear Vision' taken from *Christian Herald*, p.5, 10 June 2000

Church Mission Society and Geoff Weaver, Royal School of Church Music for the song 'Light has Come' © CMS. Tape recorded by Dr Mark Nikkel. Song composed by Rev. Moses Makur at Dhiaukuei, Southern Sudan, in 1992.

Asian Institute for Liturgy and Music, PO Box 3167, Manila, Philippines, for song 'Tanglaw (Light of God)' taken from *Masdan, O Yahweh* (AILM, 1990. AILM Collection of Church Music no.15)

Iona Community for the songs 'Imela', 'Santo', 'Jesuve Saranam', 'Many and Great', 'We are Marching (Siyahamba)'; copyright © WGRG, Iona Community, Glasgow G51 3UU, Scotland

Shrimati Susanna, South Indian Classical Dancer for the video clip of the 'Dance of the Ten Lepers' from the video *The Language of Indian Dance*

Church Mission Society for 'India' from *God's Everywhere People*

Theme 3

Church Mission Society for Requirements for Mission Partners, Job File, Link Letter of Eric and Sushila Alexander, and 'From Boy Slave to Bishop' from *God's Everywhere People*

Daniel L. Schutte and New Dawn Music for the hymn 'I, the Lord of sea and sky'; © 1981, Daniel L. Schutte and New Dawn Music, 5536 NE Hassalo, Portland, OR 97213, USA, All rights reserved. Used with permission.

BMS World Mission for the photograph of Kate and Simon Harry

Syndics of Cambridge University Library for the photograph 'The deputation who marched 60 miles in 24 hours from Kongwa to Dodoma on the outbreak of war in 1914'. Taken from the Westgate Collection of the Royal Commonwealth Society Photographic Collection in Cambridge by permission of the Syndics of Cambridge University Library.

Kate and Simon Harry and Sebastian and Kirsten Kim for their photographs

Theme 4

Ram Gidoomal for the photograph of himself taken from *Agapé News*, Summer 2000

GLS Publishing for the Staines family photographs taken from *Burnt Alive* by Vishal Mangalwadi et al (Mumbai, India, GLS Publishing, 1999)

Rev. Dr Andrew Wingate for permission to use material from *The Church and Conversion* by Andrew Wingate (New Delhi, Indian SPCK, 1997)

Church Mission Society for reference material for drawings on Stimulus Sheet 4.5

Theme 5

Johannes Merz for two photographs of African diviners from Benin © J. Merz

Theme 6

Hodder and Stoughton Limited for extract from Proverbs 31 vv.13–24, 27–28. Scripture quotations taken from the HOLY BIBLE, NEW INTERNATIONAL VERSION. Copyright © 1973, 1978, 1984 by International Bible Society. Used by permission of Hodder and Stoughton Limited, a member of the Hodder Headline Plc Group. All rights reserved. 'NIV' is a registered trademark of the International Bible Society. UK trademark number 1448790

Orbis Books for 'Madam and the other woman'. Quotes taken from *Daughters of Anowa: African Women and Patriarchy* by Mercy Oduyoye (Maryknoll, New York, Orbis Books, 1995) pp.144–6

The Most Rev. Dr David M. Gitari, Archbishop of Kenya and Bishop of Nairobi for quotes from the article 'The Church and Polygamy' by David Gitari in *Transformation* 1:1, January 1984, p.9

Church House Publishing for the quote from *The Truth Shall Make You Free: the Lambeth Conference* 1988 (London, Church House Publishing for the Anglican Consultative Council, 1988) pp.220–21

Every effort has been made to trace copyright holders. If we have failed to succeed in this, we apologize and invite those concerned to contact us.